SMALL SCALE BIG CHANGE

New Architectures of Social Engagement

Andres Lepik

The Museum of Modern Art,
New York

Birkhäuser,
Basel

Published in conjunction with the exhibition *Small Scale, Big Change: New Architectures of Social Engagement*, October 3, 2010–January 3, 2011, at The Museum of Modern Art, New York, organized by Andres Lepik, Curator, Department of Architecture and Design.

The exhibition is supported in part by The International Council of The Museum of Modern Art. Research and travel support was provided by the Patricia Cisneros Travel Fund for Latin America.

Produced by the Department of Publications, The Museum of Modern Art, New York

Edited by Libby Hruska
Designed by Project Projects
Production by Marc Sapir
Printed and bound by Sing Cheong Printing Company, Hong Kong

This book is typeset in Galaxie Copernicus (Chester Jenkins and Kris Sowersby, 2009), Galaxie Polaris (Chester Jenkins, 2004), and Saint-Sauveur (José Albergaria and Rik Bas Backer, 2009). The paper is 150 gsm Mori Silk and 100 gsm IKPP Woodfree.

Library of Congress Control Number: 2010930254

Bibliographic information Published by the German National Library: The German National Library lists this publication in the Deutsche Nationalbibliografie; detailed bibliographic data is available on the Internet at http://dnb.d-nb.de.
MoMA ISBN: 978-0-87070-784-1
Birkhäuser ISBN: 978-3-0346-0588-5

Published by
The Museum of Modern Art
11 West 53 Street, New York, NY 10019-5497
www.moma.org

Distributed in the United States and Canada by D.A.P./Distributed Art Publishers, 155 Sixth Avenue, 2nd floor, New York, NY 10013
www.artbook.com

Distributed outside the United States and Canada by Birkhäuser GmbH
P.O. Box 133, CH-4010 Basel, Switzerland
www.birkhauser-architecture.com

Cover: Diébédo Francis Kéré. Primary School. Gando, Burkina Faso. 1999–2001
Front endpaper: Map by Adrian Kitzinger

Printed in Hong Kong

6   Foreword
     Glenn D. Lowry

7   Introduction
     Barry Bergdoll

12   Building on Society
     Andres Lepik

     Projects
     Andres Lepik and
     Margot Weller

23   METI – Handmade School
     Rudrapur, Bangladesh
     Anna Heringer

33   Primary School
     Gando, Burkina Faso
     Diébédo Francis Kéré

43   Housing for the Fishermen of Tyre
     Tyre, Lebanon
     Hashim Sarkis A.L.U.D.

53   Red Location Museum of Struggle
     Port Elizabeth, South Africa
     Noero Wolff Architects

63   Inner-City Arts
     Los Angeles, California
     Michael Maltzan Architecture

73   $20K House VIII (Dave's House)
     Newbern, Alabama
     Rural Studio, Auburn University

83   Quinta Monroy Housing
     Iquique, Chile
     Elemental

93   Casa Familiar: Living Rooms
     at the Border and Senior Housing
     with Childcare
     San Ysidro, California
     Estudio Teddy Cruz

103 Transformation of Tour Bois-le-Prêtre
     Paris, France
     Frédéric Druot, Anne Lacaton,
     and Jean Philippe Vassal

113 Manguinhos Complex
     Rio de Janeiro, Brazil
     Jorge Mario Jáuregui/
     Metrópolis Projetos Urbanos

123 Metro Cable
     Caracas, Venezuela
     Urban-Think Tank

133 Project Credits

138 Acknowledgments

140 Trustees of The Museum
     of Modern Art

FOREWORD

————————

Small Scale, Big Change: New Architectures of Social Engagement invites an aspect of architecture back to The Museum of Modern Art's exhibition program that was inextricably linked with the development of early modern architecture: social relevance. From Le Corbusier's concept for Maison Dom-Ino (1914–15) to Oscar Stonorov and Alfred Kastner's Carl Mackley Houses (Philadelphia, 1933), an important part of the modern movement has always been guided by the vision of creating a better society through architecture.

The history of the Museum's engagement with promoting modern architecture has long been bound up with a sometimes reductively interpreted notion of an aestheticizing search for modern style, something associated with the supposed single-minded pursuit of the visual agenda of Henry Russell Hitchcock, Philip Johnson, and Alfred Barr's concept of the International Style. The Museum's seminal exhibition of 1932 introducing that style, which gave birth to a Department of Architecture (combined in 1949 with the Department of Industrial Design to form today's Department of Architecture and Design), was the first in a long series of exhibitions to include a focus on higher standards for public housing. Those organized together with Lewis Mumford and Catherine Bauer in the 1930s were to have a substantial influence on municipal and federal housing policy, but the tradition would continue even into the 1970s, when Arthur Drexler both responded to and helped to fuel the critique of orthodox heroic modernism, notably in an exhibition titled *Another Chance for Housing*, presented in 1973. In introducing the book that accompanied the exhibition, Drexler wrote that the Museum "recognizes—indeed it insists—that architecture even more than the other arts is bound up with ethics, social justice, technology, politics, and finance, along with the lofty desire to improve the human condition." His words are worth repeating in introducing this volume, which looks far beyond MoMA's home city to the global society of which we are now all a part.

With recent exhibitions such as *Home Delivery: Fabricating the Modern Dwelling* and *Rising Currents: Projects for New York's Waterfront*, the Architecture and Design Department has again widened its lens to consider aspects beyond aesthetic issues in the complex art of architecture. With this exhibition, organized by Andres Lepik, Curator, Department of Architecture and Design, and Margot Weller, Curatorial Assistant, MoMA reasserts its commitment to architecture that is fully engaged with and informed by its community and place. The outstanding architects included here, who embody the original spirit of the avant-garde both in its social sense and its commitment to finding an architecture of its time, together encourage a reconsideration of the roles and responsibilities of the designer in the twenty-first century.

For its support of this endeavor, I extend my sincere thanks to The International Council of The Museum of Modern Art. I am particularly grateful to the Patricia Cisneros Travel Fund for Latin America Research for providing travel support for this project.

Glenn D. Lowry
Director, The Museum of Modern Art

INTRO-DUCTION

Barry Bergdoll

Architectural modernism, and with it the mission of The Museum of Modern Art's Department of Architecture, was forged in avant-garde ambitions. Integral to this was an elevated status for the architect as visionary, master planner of cities and territories—in certain visions, even of the planet—in ways pursued in previous centuries only by all-powerful rulers from pharaohs to emperors (and twentieth-century dictators). This calling was also dreamed of by Freemasons, who imagined a role for the architect as free agent rather than servant of the state, and who took their design metaphors from a series of creation myths as well as from the image of the divine structuring of the universe—a complete and perfect system. This view of the architect's role, often laced with technocratic utopianism, was perhaps most clearly embodied in Le Corbusier's appeal for a system of modern architecture that was integral to a unified urban vision (fig. 1). Central to this were his five points of a new architecture—design elements that included raising buildings on pilotis and the ample provision of roof gardens—principles at once urban and architectural. For the Corbusian avant-garde, architecture and the large-scale reconstruction of the urban sphere were integral one to another: the comprehensive transformation of the built environment was implicit in each building block, and a brave new world was anticipated by each new fragment.

With the formation, in 1928, of the Congrès international d'architecture moderne (CIAM), an organization that brought together architects devoted to a holistic vision of the task of architecture, that all-encompassing ethos found both a rallying point and a codification, most notably in the Athens Charter. Drafted in 1933, and published a decade later, that influential document epitomizes the modernist ideal of the architect as the designer not of individual structures but of the whole framework of life. CIAM rapidly forged a highly influential consensus, one that not only motored much of the urban redevelopment of the United States, Latin America, and Western (and to a certain extent Eastern) Europe after the devastation of World War II, but which was in turn exported around much of the globe, shaping urbanization even in Africa and Asia in a period of rapid decolonization. While the Athens Charter was not the universal model in the postwar economic and population boom, even prominent dissenters shared in the modernist

1 Le Corbusier. Model of Plan Voisin (Paris, 1925; unrealized) with the architect's hand. Still from Pierre Chenal's film *L'Architecture d'aujourd'hui* (1930)

vision of the architect as a genius whose mandate extended to the full range of building types.[1] Frank Lloyd Wright, for example, drafted his comprehensive concept for Broadacre City (1932)—a decentralized vision of a sprawling suburbanized city dependent on the automobile—and continued to elaborate it as a template for remodeling both American built form and society at large in response to Roosevelt's New Deal. In the Soviet sphere, the great state architectural cooperatives were equally immersed in the utopian desire to restructure life through physical design.

In short, the credo of the modern movement, despite what historians now recognize as its great variety of positions and practices, was that a new architecture could ultimately serve for the large-scale transformation of the inherited order—whether the physical order of cities and suburbs or, for the most committed, the transformation of inherited social, political, and even economic structures. It is no mistake that utopian futures, be they political or architectural, are understood as "blueprints," a technological form of reproducing architectural plans that first found widespread use in the late nineteenth century, even as plans for wholesale building of highly structured new cities and the restructuring of existing ones began to proliferate.

For at least two generations now, this broad legacy of sweeping change has been under attack by architects and non-architects alike. Critiques of the modernist dream of remaking the world arguably began with demands for more attention to individual needs rather than simply planning for abstract social groups, and were soon followed by pressing calls to respond to the ecological and demographic crises that gained force in the late 1960s and early 1970s. An aestheticizing critique also emerged as a rallying point beginning in 1964, when Bernard Rudofsky mounted the exhibition *Architecture Without Architects* at The Museum of Modern Art (fig. 2). Rudofsky's show, which traveled to more than eighty venues over the next two decades, was accompanied by a gentle manifesto (two years before Robert Venturi would coin that term) for a "non-pedigree architecture," one in which the old dream of an organic relationship between lifestyle and landscape leads to a homegrown architecture. This call synthesized a century-old fascination concerning a protomodern vernacular architecture with the critique of the hubris of heroic authorship that so often accompanied the modern movement's vision of the architect. Further, the political and social ferment of

2 Installation view of the exhibition *Architecture Without Architects*, November 11, 1964–February 7, 1965, The Museum of Modern Art, New York

the 1960s fueled a growing conviction that the modernization project itself had failed to cope with the ever-growing wealth disparity worldwide or to provide tools for addressing social inequality and injustice.

Even more significant than direct challenges to the profession, however, has been the steady erosion of the real power of architects as shapers of the environment. As the ebbs and flows of globalization have brought both development and its discontents to nearly every corner of the planet, the role of the architect in the spatial arrangements of global capital and the concomitant commodification of space have been left largely undetermined. One could almost say, without much exaggeration, that the larger project of modernization, to which architectural modernism hitched its cart in its heroic years, has increasingly developed in a way that has had little need for the critical practice of architecture. In too many cases, the role of architects in recent years has been relegated to giving form to the landscapes and cityscapes shaped by larger forces, notably of capital flows in a globalized economy. This was certainly a reality felt more than half a century ago when architects recognized that their role in the development of the American skyscraper was often reduced to dressing the frame designed by engineers and developers.

The postmodernist critique on the sometimes naive, sometimes hubristic heroics of the modern movement—formulated analytically, for instance, in the theoretical writings of Robert Venturi and Denise Scott Brown and famously parodied in Tom Wolfe's influential *From Bauhaus to Our House* of 1981—has meant that the social potential of the modernist project has too often in recent decades been thrown out with the bathwater of grand aspirations. Postmodernism might be said to have been a project of divide and conquer. In the 1980s, especially, pluralism was celebrated over doctrine. This position was all too often accompanied by a studied apolitical stance, often in the guise of a rejection of discredited political positions of earlier generations. While postmodernism's hold in the schools of architecture, particularly in European and American schools central to the honing of each generation's architectural discourse, was short-lived, stylistic postmodernism's formal languages— of reviving familiar and comforting aspects of traditional architectural styles, often with a witty hyperbolism— have lived on in much commercial

architectural practice. But a backlash had already begun in the academy, meaning that politically engaged architectural practices have, since the late 1980s, tended to focus on the critical exposure of underlying ideological structures of architectural practice. As architecture focused more on functioning like the other arts— as an instrument for altering vision and frames of mind—and celebrated more frequently the designer as artist and theorist rather than as partner of the client or future inhabitant, the radical potential of transformative architecture was harnessed more for critical practices than pragmatic social engagement.

It was in the wake of the radical aestheticism of much postmodernism, particularly in its North American version, that a number of groups came together to recover something of the lost larger projects of modernism— on the one hand its ambitions to be integral with territorial planning, on the other its social commitment. Almost simultaneously, various movements sought to redefine a community-based architecture on vastly different terms. One of the most influential critiques of modernist orthodoxy, known as New Urbanism, launched in the early 1980s and constituted since 1993 in the Congress of New Urbanists, a traditionalist sort of CIAM, seeks to forge an alliance between development and an architecture—generally very conservative in formal expression— that can serve to rewrite not only the look of new urban and suburban developments worldwide but also the codes by which such developments are produced. Nearly diametrically opposed was Architects for Social Responsibility, founded in 1982. Not surprisingly finding its first adherents in Berkeley, California, the group seeks to recover the lost social conscience of architecture with an agenda—largely more an ethical code than specific design criteria—for instilling a sense of responsibility for the consequences of design.

A potential middle ground can be found in the now largely forgotten efforts from the late 1970s and 1980s

of participatory architecture. Pioneered in Scandinavia as early as the 1930s and in Britain and Australia in the 1960s, the movement gained ground on both sides of the Atlantic, led by several influential teaching architects who also had aspirations to maintain high standards of authorial design: Charles Moore and his partners John Ruble and Buzz Yudell in the United States; Ralph Erskine in the United Kingdom and Sweden; and Lucien Kroll in Belgium, among others. Such practitioners provided potent models of architecture with a dynamic give-and-take between designer and users in the crafting of a transformed and transformative environment, although those experiments of the 1970s and '80s, once widely discussed as new paradigms for practice involving workshops with future users, have today been largely forgotten with the rise, since the 1980s, of the persona of the "starchitect"—a single designing genius more related to the economics of haute couture than to the old Masonic dream of the architect as giver of master blueprints.

In the United States, Lawrence Halprin, a sometime collaborator with Moore, notably on the seminal Sea Ranch project (1965), extended this credo of involving the end user in the design process into landscape design. (His most famous urban parks have been the subject of much critique, however, and several works have even been demolished, including Skyline Park in Denver.) It is worth remembering the ethos of Halprin's stance vis-à-vis the legacy of modernism: "To be properly understood, Modernism is not just a matter of cubist space but of a whole appreciation of environmental design as a holistic approach to the matter of making spaces for people to live.... Modernism, as I define it and practice it, *includes* and is based on the vital archetypal needs of human beings as individuals as well as social groups."[2]

It is against this backdrop that the ambitions of *Small Scale, Big Change: New Architectures of Social Engagement* must be understood. The implicit critiques of the architects included here build on aspects of those formulated since the 1960s, even as they develop a wholly twenty-first-century vision. Many today—practitioners and critics alike—are rediscovering the critiques of orthodox modernism of the 1970s, and rethinking them afresh in relationship to challenges, both environmental and social, that seem exponentially more pressing forty years later. Experiments of three and four decades ago, which were largely dismissed in the heady, go-go economy of the 1990s and early naughts, are being scrutinized as unfinished experiments—lost opportunities to be learned from and extended. A brilliant exhibition at the Canadian Centre for Architecture, *1973: Sorry, Out of Gas* (2007), brought to light a whole series of practices and proposals from the 1970s that responded to the worldwide oil crisis of 1973. That crisis gave an impetus to environmentalism, to searches for energy conservation and ecological design, and to a new relationship to nature, all of which no longer seem to be quaint exper-iments in the face of ever-escalating demands for a finite quantity of fossil fuels, the perils of oil dependency revealed by the fiasco in the Gulf of Mexico, and ever-increasing evidence of long-term climate change.[3] At the same time, the demographic explosion, particularly evident in shantytowns worldwide—from São Paulo to Mumbai, from Cairo to Jakarta—whose populations continue to swell, has added renewed urgency to the search for innovative solutions for the proliferation of slum-dwelling worldwide. Philanthropic support has reached new heights, and private entities are now engaging in activities previously confined largely to government agencies and the United Nations.[4] There is a prevailing sense that the goal now is, in the words of Sheela Patel, chair of the board of Shack/Slum Dwellers International, for "poor communities to demonstrate to their municipalities, governments and international development agen-cies that self-organized communities of the poor are partners in addressing urban poverty."[5] Here we have come

a full 180 degrees from the modernist belief in the architect as an all-seeing deus ex machina.

This more collaborative attitude is shared by most of the architects included here, who have developed new models of architectural practice that echo this conviction, but who also believe—as has not always been the case—that excellent architecture need not be abandoned in the process. There is an overarching sense that both the persona of the architect and the strategy for creating architecture should not resign itself to simply decorating the forms of settlement and development determined by economic, political, and social forces and accepted as the status quo. The position is potent, even if the group here does not seek in any way to constitute a new doctrine, write a new manual, gather together a worldwide network of adherents, or change the world through large-scale gestures. While some have formed schools and institutes, they have not created a singular theory or code of practice. Further, they often work in multiple modes, undertaking for-profit responses to briefs offered by individuals, government bodies, or competitions, all the while extending their role as agent in a series of discrete interventions that offer a definition of what it means to be an architect in the twenty-first century.

While many of their concerns are reminiscent of the socially engaged movements in architecture of the last great moment of prolonged economic uncertainty, they have a new model of empowerment of local communities that goes beyond the consultative models developed a generation ago. Their conception of design extends beyond undertaking a building or a site plan to devising procedures for getting things to happen where there are no such procedures in place, and to creating new models of involvement for local populations. Change is something that happens incrementally, in the view of this multigenerational group, some of whose practices—as in the case of Jorge Mario Jáuregui in Rio de Janeiro—reach back nearly

two decades, others of whom have been in practice for just a few years. Situations are improved not by eradicating what already exists but through implantation of a different set of possibilities, whether it be something as simple as a school or an arts center or a more rigorous urban intervention such as the insertion of a cable car into one of Caracas's most notorious hillside barrios. Increasingly, the group's efforts are gaining official recognition, not only in the form of prizes from the architectural profession but in invitations to work in partnership with governments and other established entities.

On one level, such self-con-sciously marginal practices for marginal clients has a high degree of pragmatism that might seem to be the final collapse of the historic avant-garde in architecture, with its belief in large-scale progress and the role of architecture in structuring a world to come. In this these architects may be criticized for their willingness to allow larger forces of social injustice to remain intact, and for accepting that the architect can only act in isolated, local interventions. But in extending the notion of "architectural acupuncture"—most cogently elaborated in the late 1990s in the transformation of the inherited urban fabric of Barcelona by Manuel de Solà Morales[6]—to the developing world and to populations long deprived of architectural services, these architects have elaborated a position for the contemporary practitioner that has more in common with the theory of microfinance or the idea of the legal clinics for the poor than it does with the participatory or activist architecture of the 1970s, or for that matter with church-based organizations such as Habitat for Humanity, which have rarely considered architectural quality a criterion in their quest for providing shelter to those who need it most. One important lesson to draw from these architects as they work against both the forces and the assumptions of globalization, is that the flow of knowledge can move in multiple directions, that new perceptions about the needs of a severely challenged developed world can be found in practices developed in the underdeveloped world, particularly as the issue of appropriate technology becomes the most urgent mantra for architectural practice everywhere, from the villages of Burkina Faso to the five boroughs of New York City.

One might ask if the approaches put forth here represent the final death of the avant-garde or a return to its transformative aspirations. It was the original Saint-Simonians, the nineteenth-century social utopians, who first transferred the terminology of the "avant-garde" or "vanguard" from the language of military operations to a notion of the artist as one who saw clearly what was ahead and sought to address and ameliorate it. The first uses of the term avant-garde to refer to an artistic posture were in the 1820s in Paris, and one of the first to respond was the architect Henri Labrouste, who in 1830 wrote to his fellow architectural rebel Louis Duc that he would like to think of the architect as a kind of doctor for society, since he believed the arts could have an influence even on public health, and by extension on the overall health of the society.[7] And like the visionary role for the architect that the avant-garde presupposed, the architects included in this volume might be applauded for their commitment to realities of great urgency long before the current global economic downturn made these necessities painfully obvious to nearly the entire globe. They do not propose a single universal truth in architecture to the exclusion of other positions. Rather, they champion an activism that has little time for manifestos, preferring to channel energies into the realization of small projects that have an immediate impact on their environments. Though they have generally operated as individuals, these architects nonetheless represent an emerging sensibility that reverberates with the larger question of where architecture stands against

the larger forces that shape the environment today. If indeed a nascent movement is afoot here, it has as its central tenet that a matter-of-fact pragmatism of small-scale intervention can have an outsize influence on life in rural Alabama, the outskirts of Paris, or a barrio in Caracas.

1   For more on CIAM, see Eric Mumford, *The CIAM Discourse on Urbanism, 1928-1960* (Cambridge, Mass.: The MIT Press, 2001; and Robert Fishman, *Urban Utopias of the Twentieth Century: Ebenezer Howard, Frank Lloyd Wright, and Le Corbusier* (New York: Basic Books, 1977).

2   Quoted in Peter Walker and Melanie Simo, *Invisible Gardens: The Search for Modernism in the American Landscape* (Cambridge, Mass.: The MIT Press, 1994), p. 9.

3   Mirko Zardini, "Think Different," in *Sorry, Out of Gas: Architecture's Response to the 1973 Oil Crisis*, ed. Giovanna Borasi and Mirko Zardini (Montreal: Canadian Centre for Architecture, 2007).

4   In 2007, for example, the Bill and Melinda Gates Foundation announced a grant of $10 million to the nongovernmental organization Shack/Slum Dwellers International to support actions to improve housing, water provision, and sanitation to the urban poor in Africa, Asia, and Latin America.

5   International Institute for Environment and Development, "Gates Foundation gives US$10 million to help urban poor improve living conditions," http://www.iied. org/human-settlements/media/ gates-foundation-gives-us10- million-help-urban-poor-improve- living-conditions.

6   Manuel de Solà Morales, *Progettare città/Designing Cities, Lotus Quaderni/Documents*, no. 23, ed. Mirko Zardini (Milan: Electa, 1999). Cited in Kenneth Frampton, *Labour, Work, and Architecture: Collected Essays on Architecture and Design* (London: Phaidon, 2002), p. 16.

7   Henri Labrouste, "Lettres inédites sur l'enseignement de l'architecture (Paris, 1830-31)," *La Construction moderne* 9 (March 1895): 268-69.

BUILDING ON SOCIETY

Andres Lepik

Architecture can be a powerful instrument to affect social change. On a small scale, a well-designed school can positively influence individual learning and help children to identify themselves as parts of a larger community. On a larger scale, urban planning that offers not only the basic requirements of housing, transportation, and commerce but also parks, public squares, and cultural facilities can increase the quality of life for all inhabitants, bolster civic pride, and have a positive impact on a city's economy. But successful architecture—that which transcends the barest requirements to create a place of usefulness and beauty—is far from reaching all segments of global society, including large parts of the population that do not even have housing that meets basic needs. According to the United Nations, roughly one billion of the world's population of some 6.75 billion people live in extreme poverty, with an income of less than $150 per year and limited access to clean water, education, and health care.[1] The ongoing challenges faced by these segments of the population are occasionally brought to the world's attention, highlighted by catastrophic events such as the tsunami that hit Southeast Asia in 2004 and the earthquakes that devastated Sichuan province in China in 2008 and Haiti in early 2010. In addition to the obvious human tragedy wrought by such disasters, there is also the immediate toll on the built environment—homes, schools, hospitals, even entire neighborhoods and villages destroyed or rendered unusable. In many cases, poor construction,

or buildings that were not adjusted to local hazards, can be the cause of even more destruction. Lack of access to adequate housing and infrastructure is not, of course, limited to developing countries. By most measures, inequality in the distribution of income and wealth in the developed world continues to grow, leading to vast disparities in the living conditions of large segments of society.

Faced with such challenges in our built environment, questions inevitably arise regarding the role of the architect at the beginning of the twenty-first century: is it enough to simply be a service provider who works solely to fulfill commissions for clients who can afford such services? What proportion of the world's population is good architecture reaching today? How can architects use their training for the greater good? Worldwide, a large number of organizations are engaged in building shelters for victims of emergencies and war zones, while others are building schools, clinics, and orphanages in areas of need. But most of these initiatives are focused on the functional requirements of such structures. Architecture that is carefully designed, responds to cultural nuance, adds aesthetic value, and facilitates new or better communication within a community, is by necessity rarely a priority for these programs.

The recent global economic crisis—which arguably began with the crash of the u.s. housing market—has heightened the perception that architecture of the past few decades has placed itself too much in the service of economic and political interests and has had too little regard for social concerns. With the rapid proliferation of high-end architecture in fast-growing economies around the globe and the powerful reshaping of cities such as Dubai, architects began to be seen more and more through the lens of celebrity.

Combating poverty, hunger, inadequate medical care, politically and economically motivated migration, lack of education, and inhumane

living conditions, especially on a large scale, undoubtedly requires action at the political level. Yet architects are, in increasing numbers, using their knowledge and skills to offer well-designed solutions to localized problems. *Small Scale, Big Change: New Architectures of Social Engagement* presents eleven projects that, taken together, offer a redefining of the architect's role in and responsibility to society. These undertakings, developed independently of each other in nine countries on five continents, aim to provide lasting solutions to specific needs. They are not intended to solve large, systemic problems by applying preconceived political theories or utopian concepts. Instead, each has identified a specific need and set out to meet it, whether in conjunction with a local nongovernmental organization or a larger city initiative. The active participation of the community lends these endeavors additional value. Each project is the result of a dialogue in which the architect cedes parts of his or her authority to others, marking an important departure from the modernist ideal of the architect as a mastermind who designs everything from teapots to entire metropolises. By reevaluating the role they play, these architects are signaling their conviction that good design is not a privilege of the few and powerful. Just as the notion of microcredit, developed by Bangladeshi economist Muhammad Yunus in the 1970s, has emerged as one important way to provide the poorest of citizens a chance to succeed, the practitioners and projects highlighted here demonstrate that in architecture, too, smaller endeavors can have great consequences.

Materiality

Just as it is vital to understand the needs of a given community before designing a building, it is also important to understand what building materials and techniques are viable for a given area. This is especially true in smaller towns and villages in developing countries, where there is often a lack of heavy machinery and energy for construction on an industrial level. In such places, building with materials such as concrete, steel, and glass makes far less sense than turning to more traditional modes. Building with earth, for example, is one of mankind's oldest construction methods, and it includes various methods from rammed earth to mud bricks.[2] This tradition, which dates back to the first settlements in Mesopotamia, has roots that reach into the early decades of the twentieth century, not only in developing countries but also in Europe and the United States. In the 1930s, for example, the U.S. government supported a small program that was devoted to rammed-earth building in Gardendale, Alabama, and it successfully built seven houses, which are still standing.[3] The idea of building with earth was even embraced by masters of modernist architecture such as Frank Lloyd Wright and Le Corbusier, both of whom experimented in the 1940s with rammed-earth walls and compressed-earth blocks in plans for affordable-housing projects.[4] Despite such examples, however, over the course of the twentieth century this technique has for the most part been stigmatized as backward or primitive.

For her METI-Handmade School in Rudrapur, Bangladesh (pp. 23–32), architect Anna Heringer employed molded-earth, or cob, building as the primary technique.[5] When she began her proposal for the school, Heringer, who had spent several extended periods of time in the village, knew that she wanted to utilize cob—a mixture of mud, straw, and water long used throughout the region. Rather than being formed into bricks and dried, cob walls are shaped by hand in layers, lending the final structure a sculptural effect. Though she was consciously reintroducing a traditional technology, Heringer also improved on the technique by placing her molded walls on concrete foundations, altering the mixture of materials to make it more durable, and building a roof structure out of bamboo that also creates a full second floor of usable space.

Heringer learned about the advantages of rammed-earth building in a class taught by Martin Rauch at the University for Arts and Industrial Design in Linz, Austria. Rauch has been specializing in earth building for more than twenty years. He has also spent time in Africa as a development aid worker, which has helped him to understand the challenges of working in remote areas. In 1984 he won the first prize in a competition for low-cost housing models in Africa, for which he developed an improved technology for building with clay. Since the 1990s, he has been building projects around the world using various earth-building technologies. Heringer, hoping to draw on this depth of knowledge, asked Rauch if he would travel to Rudrapur to consult on the right mixture of materials and precise building methods for her project.

Heringer's school as well as the projects that have followed—village housing and a vocational school for electrical training—have made a significant impact on the village of Rudrapur and beyond by arousing new interest in the use of local, easily sourced materials. In March 2009 Heringer and Rauch, along with the Housing and Building Research Institute of Bangladesh, were invited to present a workshop on modern earthen structures and sustainable architecture in the country's capital, Dhaka. The popular course, organized by the Institute of Architects Bangladesh, introduced more than seventy prominent architects, engineers, and students to technical and structural innovations in earth-building, a vital step in rekindling interest in this time-honored and ecologically sound building tradition.

Diébédo Francis Kéré is another architect who has focused on using materials and developing building strategies that are related to local craftsmanship and traditions. His primary school in Gando, Burkina Faso (pp. 33–42)—Kéré's home village—is constructed of sun-dried mud bricks, the very material used in and around the village for virtually all building needs. Kéré's design, however, introduced improvements to the traditional bricks used throughout the country, including using a man-powered machine to compress the bricks more than usual, and, like Heringer, slightly altering their content to make them more stable and resistant to rain. Kéré's approach also presents an opportunity for local workers and craftsmen, who learned new skills during the building of the school, including the making of the compressed bricks and how to lay foundations, which they can apply to future projects. The transfer of information, however, flows in two directions. Kéré, who teaches at the Technical University in Berlin, has since 2005 regularly brought his students to Gando for site visits and workshops. These architects-in-training learn firsthand how complex the development and realization of building projects in such a rural and remote setting can be.

Of course these and other such initiatives are not the first to apply ancient building techniques in contemporary ways. One of the most influential modern practitioners of this approach was Egyptian architect Hassan Fathy. By the 1940s, Fathy was arguing against the use of industrial materials such as steel and concrete as well as the use of heavy machinery, instead advocating more traditional means of building. Fathy was instrumental in bringing public attention to the importance of using mud bricks and other earth-building techniques as inexpensive solutions to the housing shortage in rural Egypt.

Fathy's most renowned project was the village of New Gourna, a complex commissioned by the Egyptian government that was to include housing, markets, schools, and more (fig. 1). The new quarters were to house the seven thousand residents of Gourna who the

government planned to relocate after it was discovered that members of the community had been looting the ancient pharaonic tombs of Luxor, above which their village was located.[6] Fathy saw his design for New Gourna, which was built between 1945 and 1947, as a chance to develop a new paradigm for rural development. He rigorously studied the traditional housing typology of the area and worked with villagers to understand their specific needs. He recognized that the project would only succeed with the participation of the future users in the planning and construction. And, as always, his design eschewed highly industrialized building technologies, instead utilizing mud bricks and reintroducing the Nubian vault technique, a method for vaulting spaces without the use of timber. With his book on New Gourna, published in 1973 in English as *Architecture for the Poor: An Experiment in Rural Egypt*, he gained a wider audience, and was recognized as a forerunner of ecological and social planning.

Activist Simone Swan became enthusiastic about the social impact of the use of adobe after reading Fathy's book and following a personal encounter with him in 1976. She proceeded to work in his archive in Egypt, and traveled with him as a volunteer when he was invited

1   Hassan Fathy. New Gourna Village. New Gourna, Egypt. 1948. Theater, exterior facade

to build the Dar al Islam mosque in Abiquiú, New Mexico. After studying architectural history and researching traditional uses of adobe, in 1994 she founded the Adobe Alliance, a nonprofit organization based in the border region of western Texas, an area with an extremely high poverty rate. One of the group's main objectives is to aid communities in learning to utilize cooperative building techniques. The alliance,

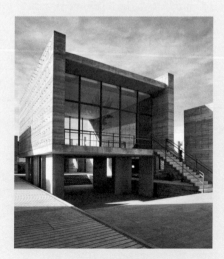

2   Taller de Arquitectura – Mauricio Rocha. School of Plastic Arts. Oaxaca, Mexico. 2007–08

which advocates the social and political aspects of earth architecture, tries to influence local building codes, which often limit the use of adobe. It also aims to educate people in how to work with traditional materials, and its biannual adobe workshops receive worldwide attention.[7] Camacho Residence, built by the alliance in 1995 in the Mexican state of Chihuahua, has served as a model of the organization's mission, both for its use of mud bricks and the extreme low cost of its erection ($5,000) and because the owner himself became an expert in mud-brick building during the construction process.[8]

Today, numerous initiatives employing such technologies can be found worldwide. The Oaxaca School of Plastic Arts in Mexico (fig. 2), designed by Taller de Arquitectura – Mauricio Rocha, which uses rammed earth for large parts of its construction, successfully merges the needs of a contemporary university setting with the benefits of traditional building. Constructed largely from material excavated during the building of this and other on-campus structures, the rammed-earth walls not only create surface interest but also help to regulate interior temperatures. In Europe, Martin Rauch, the earth-building expert discussed above, has used the technique to build everything from residences to chapels.[9] He has provided a highly regarded model with his own house in the village of Schlins, in the Austrian region of Vorarlberg (fig. 3). Examples such as this, which demonstrate that rammed-earth building is also relevant for climates with high precipitation and extreme winter temperatures, help to broaden the appreciation for the technique from the associations of dirt and poverty to a highly sustainable and adaptable technology.[10]

Creating Places of Social Identity

Underprivileged segments of society generally have no political say in the planning and building of infrastructure and community spaces.

As a result, these groups often find themselves relegated to less desirable locations without easy access to public services let alone parks, libraries, or other cultural amenities. The Red Location Museum of Struggle (pp. 53–62), in Port Elizabeth, South Africa, serves as a particularly poignant example of how architecture can play a role in commemorating even the most severe discrimination. The museum is dedicated to the history of apartheid and is the first in South Africa to be built in a township. Red Location has long been home to black industrial workers, and in the days of apartheid it was one of the major centers of organized political resistance. Architect Jo Noero, who had worked in the townships long before the end of apartheid, knew this history well even before he began his plans for the museum. He understood that the acceptance of a public building inserted into a township would depend on the meaningful involvement of the community in all phases of planning and construction, and on an architectural language that blends in with its surroundings.

Building a museum that memorializes the history of apartheid on a site so laden with meaning has a powerful symbolic resonance, but it also holds the ability to address concrete issues that continue to face the community. The museum is only the first part of a master plan that will eventually include an art museum (currently under construction), a library, a performing arts center, and a municipal archive. It is hoped that such a vibrant urban precinct will have a transformative effect on the entire area. Though since the end of apartheid the government has made an effort to provide the township with the necessary basics, such as water, electricity, and garbage collection, the local population still suffers high unemployment and extreme poverty. It is hoped that the apartheid museum and other aspects of the master plan

3 Martin Rauch. House Rauch. Schlins, Austria. 2006–07

will play a significant part in reversing some of that legacy. More than two hundred jobs were created during construction, and about seventy people are now employed by the museum in various positions. The museum currently draws about nine thousand visitors each month. As this number continues to grow, and more people begin to patronize local businesses, the expectation is that the cycle of improvement will only accelerate.

Cape Town's Dignified Places Programme, initiated by the city's Spatial Planning and Urban Design Department in 1998, is an attempt to reconcile South Africa's legacy of apartheid through the creation of public spaces in all of that city's townships. Projects were planned in conjunction with major public transportation hubs that would allow

ANDRES LEPIK

the improvements to reach the greatest number of people—and that would over time become ideal spots for the small businesses and other private initiatives that the planners hoped would follow. To date, more than ninety-seven projects, including shops and marketplaces, courthouses, schools, bus shelters, and public parks, have been installed. While there is no instant solution to the extreme poverty and other deep-seated problems these communities face, the belief is that such small interventions will, over time, improve living conditions for all residents.

Michael Maltzan's Inner-City Arts (ICA) (pp. 63–72), in Los Angeles, aims to use architecture to have a lasting influence on a very different community. ICA, a private initiative, has been providing art instruction to children from low-income families since 1989. The school is guided by the conviction that encouraging creativity in children can lead to other positive results, including gains in literacy and better academic achievement overall. It offers classes to local public schools as well as after-school and weekend programs. After holding classes in temporary locations for several years, in 1992 the purchase of an 8,000-square-foot (750-square-meter) autobody shop enabled the organization to establish a permanent home. A three-phase renovation and expansion ensued, culminating in a welcome arts facility for the neighborhood. Within this challenging context, ICA serves as a micro-urban oasis and a neighborhood magnet. Maltzan has also worked with the Skid Row Housing Trust to develop a concept for longer-term housing for the homeless. The New Carver Apartments (fig. 4), Maltzan's second collaboration with the trust, is an innovative and sophisticated response to creating housing on a particularly inhospitable parcel of land adjacent to a major highway interchange. His solution was to erect two fan-shaped buildings that curve toward one another, each containing five stories of private living spaces above communal facilities. Given the highly exposed site, thoughtfully placed windows

4   Michael Maltzan Architecture. New Carver Apartments. Los Angeles, California. 2006–09

help to mitigate concerns about noise and privacy. Because the interior courtyard is open to the sky, however, the overall effect of the design is one of openness as well as refuge. As with ICA, here Maltzan overcame a number of challenges in order to provide a hopeful space to an underserved and typically marginalized community.

Teaching by Example

Throughout the 1990s, a number of design-build programs got their start. These initiatives focus on taking students or recent graduates from the beginning planning phases of a project through construction, often with an emphasis on building for underserved communities. Those who are directly involved in practical works can take away lessons about collaborative design practices, budgeting, and hands-on experience—things that are generally not taught in architecture school. Working with marginalized communities also gives students a deeper understanding of the possible impact of their future profession. One influential program is Bryan Bell's Design Corps, established in Raleigh, North Carolina, in 1991. The studio has focused largely on providing design and building assistance to

poor, rural areas. One focus of the program has been to design mobile housing units for migrant workers in different parts of the country. In 2000 Bell organized a conference, which since 2002 has become an annual event, titled Structures for Inclusion. Through these gatherings, as well as his writings, Bell has advanced the notion that architecture has a social responsibility to an even wider audience.[11]

In 1993 Samuel Mockbee and D.K. Ruth founded Rural Studio (pp. 73–82), an offshoot of the architecture school of Auburn University, in Alabama.[12] The program was set up in an old farmhouse in Newbern, a small Hale County town roughly a three-hour drive from the university's main campus in Auburn. For Mockbee, the studio was begun as a direct reaction against the architecture of his time, which he felt was becoming more and more oblivious to social issues. His declared intention was to develop projects with his students, from housing to community centers and parks, that would benefit the poor in rural Hale County (fig. 5). Living conditions there have barely changed since James Agee and Walker Evans captured their indelible Great Depression images of poverty and hardship in the region. From the beginning, however, Mockbee was interested in providing more than simply low-cost solutions—each project was to meet a higher design standard.

Begun as a one-year experiment, the program has become a permanent institution. Since Mockbee's death in 2001, the program has been directed by Andrew Freear, a former teacher at the school. To date, Rural Studio has built more than 120 structures within a 25-mile (40-kilometer) radius. Each project has been a response to a perceived need, and was created in consultation with the people who would benefit from it. The program

5   Rural Studio. Harris/Butterfly House. Mason's Bend, Alabama. 1996

has left its mark not only on the Hale County community but also on the approximately six hundred students who have participated so far. Its influence can also be felt in the numerous programs based on its model that have been initiated elsewhere.

Hank Louis, who was inspired by a lecture Mockbee gave at the University of Utah, Salt Lake City, when he was an architecture student there, went on to found a program called DesignBuildBLUFF, also at the University of Utah. His program, begun in 2000, works with students in the Navajo Nation in southeast Utah. There is also a design-build workshop focusing on underserved communities at the Department of Housing and Design at the Vienna University of Technology. One of the program's earliest projects, in 2000, was to redesign the containers in a special transit area of Vienna's airport that houses asylum-seekers, changing the drab and poorly furnished interiors to well-designed spaces with kitchens, places to sleep, and Internet stations. In 2003, the program became active abroad as well. Among their completed projects are a day-care center and a kindergarten in a township outside of Johannesburg, South Africa. Another important educational program with a global scope is the University of Washington's Building Sustainable Communities Initiative (UW BaSiC), established by Sergio Palleroni in 1995.[13] It involves faculty and students in the development of ecologically sustainable projects both in the Seattle area and the rural regions of eastern Washington, as well as in Native American communities in the United States and in Latin America, Africa, and India. Many of the ideas behind these initiatives go back to the 1970s, when Steve Badanes founded the innovative design-build firm Jersey Devil, which traveled around the country following work wherever it was needed. Such programs show how architecture schools can furnish students with the practical experience needed to bring about social change with a combination of creativity and hard work.

New Models for Building

The past decade or so has seen a growing number of architects take a fresh look at the economics of building for the underserved. Architecture firm Elemental, for example, is redefining the perception of such work from being necessarily pro bono or charity to being a profitable enterprise. With their design for a low-income housing project in Iquique, Chile (pp. 83–92), the architects took on the challenge of building and selling a house for just $7,500—the support the Chilean government was offering for each family participating in the project, including the lot. After much experimentation, they decided this could only be achieved by building just half of each house, leaving the other half to be finished by the new occupants.[14] By making it necessary for residents to share structural elements, the growth of houses would aim to cultivate social cohesion as well. Elemental has successfully translated this business model to many other housing projects in Chile and Mexico.

For architect Teddy Cruz, a new approach to building means challenging the traditional top-down planning process, confronting bureaucratic challenges, and encouraging dialogue among local constituencies. For the past decade, Cruz has studied the relationships between social and urban structures, and his work has long focused on the issues facing unplanned settlements along the border between the United States and Mexico. He is an outspoken critic of the way architecture is typically practiced in highly developed countries, where it primarily serves financial interests. "The most inventive, progressive, experimental projects have not happened in China or the Emirates (where architecture is so often treated as an object or icon)," he has said, "but within the context of infrastructure, in Latin America."[15]

Cruz has mainly communicated his ideas through lectures, publications, and exhibitions, but now, with a project underway in the San Diego community of San Ysidro, California (pp. 93–102), he is translating them to built form. In collaboration with the community-based, nonprofit organization Casa Familiar, Cruz has developed a new concept for suburban living for a low-income immigrant community accustomed to living in close proximity with extended family. Because the existing zoning only permitted large single-family houses, meant to result in the low density typical of a suburban neighborhood, one of the basic challenges was to increase the building density allowed in the area. In order to get permission for Cruz's project, which called for multiple dwellings and mixed-use structures built on a single lot, Cruz demonstrated to the local planning agency that a well-conceived neighborhood district would be preferable to the ad hoc building currently taking place. He ultimately won approval for his plan, and construction is slated to begin in mid-2011. Cruz is currently working to apply this experience to other communities in all states along the border with Mexico.

Strategies for Slum-Upgrading

One of the greatest challenges for the future of the world's population is the unchecked spread of informal settlements, usually by the poorest of residents, in major cities and megalopolises. Historically, this growth has been virtually ignored by public policymakers. Prior to the first conference sponsored by the United Nations Human Settlements Programme, in Vancouver in 1976, it occasioned only slight political interest. City planning, especially in the countries below what Teddy Cruz has dubbed the "political equator" (fig. 6), where such settlements have

proliferated most dramatically, was traditionally defined by and for the needs of the middle and upper classes. Such planning has typically meant increasing roads for more private cars, housing built to higher technical standards, and amenities—public squares and buildings, schools, transportation, cultural facilities, and so on—designed for a population whose basic needs have more than been met. Little if any thought has been given to the massive influx into cities of the extremely poor, whether they are migrating from the countryside or arriving from another country.

These shantytowns, which in many cases are growing faster than the planned sections, are generally

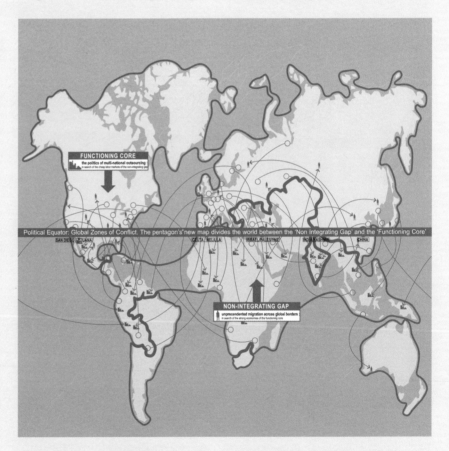

6   Estudio Teddy Cruz. Political Equator Map. 2006

densely populated, and over the years have tended to develop into close-knit communities and their own fully functioning ecosystems. But their mostly illegal status and the absence of public services has also led, in many cases, to high crime rates and a general lack of security. For these

and other reasons, the early 1990s saw a change in political thinking. Governments came to accept the idea that illegal, improvised settlements should no longer be simply tolerated—or excluded altogether—but rather recognized as established fact and gradually incorporated into the larger urban context.[16] Cities such as Rio de Janeiro and São Paulo, for example, began to experiment with ways to link favelas to their urban cores, while still preserving established social structures to the extent possible. One vital starting point is extending infrastructure and basic services. It is also necessary to give the settlements permanent legal status, so that their inhabitants enjoy the security of being

able to stay in the structures they have built themselves. Given the explosive growth of such areas, however, improvement in living conditions will come only gradually at best.

The Favela-Bairro Project in Rio de Janeiro represents one successful strategy for assisting that city's innumerable favelas. The program, which was established by the city government with support from the Inter-American Development Bank, was directed by architect Jorge Mario Jáuregui. It was based on the idea of offering a number of smaller measures, for example providing communal laundry facilities and day-care centers, a meeting place for the elderly, paving streets and building stairways, and erecting sports complexes, with the hope that these amenities might lead to swift but essential improvements in local living conditions. Where it was necessary to remove shacks for new buildings, nearby replacement housing was provided (fig. 7).[17] A basic element of this program was to create an infrastructure to support sanitation services, such as drop-off points for garbage that can be reached by carts. Actual building was accompanied by other measures, including the gradual legalization of the remodeled settlements and the creation of

additional social welfare programs. It is estimated by the city's officials that the program reached some 450,000 inhabitants in 105 favelas, and it served as the model for the Bairro Legal project in São Paulo. In 2008, when the funding of the Favela-Bairro program ended, Jáuregui was given the contract for the Manguinhos Complex (pp. 113–22) in Rio, located in a large area, encompassing some ten favelas, known for its extremely high crime rate. While the Favela-Bairro Project was based on the idea of improvement through small interventions, the Manguinhos Complex is a much more ambitious project that aims to completely transform a large urban site.

Jáuregui, who was born in Argentina and moved to Brazil for political reasons in 1978, began studying the urban divide in Rio in the 1980s. He has long been concerned with how illegal settlements can be integrated into the rest of the city so as to begin to bridge the divide between the two populations. He began by conducting intensive research within the favelas, talking

7 Jorge Mario Jáuregui Architects. Favela-Bairro Project. Rio de Janeiro. 1995–2003. Macacos Relocation Building (2001)

with their inhabitants and coming to an understanding of their specific circumstances. "The *favelados* live in an absolutely precarious situation," Jáuregui has said. "Any proposal for an improvement of their living conditions, to give them a small place is better than the present situation, and is welcome. But the most important question is to go further than to introduce an infrastructure, ways and services. All this is necessary, but the most important thing is to configure with all these elements a new 'aura' of place."[18] With each new project he brings considerable experience that allows him to effectively address the particular issues faced by these communities.

Urban-Think Tank is another firm that believes small steps can ultimately add up to a great improvement. The founders of the firm, Alfredo Brillembourg and Hubert Klumpner, first developed

their suggestions for improving the shantytowns of Caracas based on their own research. In 2004, with the construction of the Gimnasio Vertical (fig. 8), a three-story sports center next to one of the inner-city barrios, Barrio La Cruz, Urban-Think Tank was able to realize one of its ideas: to create new social facilities while keeping the high density of the neighborhood and not demolishing or forcing people to leave their houses. Its aim was to provide young people a wider range of sports options than the single soccer field they had before. Thanks to its broad offerings, the new center, available to the barrio's inhabitants at no cost virtually around the clock,

has been an overwhelming success. The building was designed to make use of simple materials, and presents a sturdy, no-nonsense appearance. The division of space is functional, and allows great flexibility. This project began with a long-term conversation with the community, community leaders, and the representatives of the urban district. Due to its success, the model of the Gimnasio Vertical has since been adopted by other sections of the city.

Since 2003 Urban-Think Tank has been working on a much larger-scale intervention that aims to address the physical divides between barrios and urban cores. Metro Cable

8   Urban-Think Tank with M. M. Pinto. Gimnasio Vertical, Chacao Prototype. Caracas, Venezuela. 2001–03

(pp. 123–32), which opened in 2010, is an aerial tramway that connects the barrio San Agustín, perched in the hills high above Caracas, to the city below. Previously, this area had been disconnected from the services and amenities of the city by a six-lane highway and a river with only one footbridge. The project was initially designed by Brillembourg and Klumpner in 2003, but did not receive the necessary approval from the government until 2007.

The original concept, which included cultural facilities and other services to be placed at each of the stops on the line, and additional community sports centers in the favela, has only been partially realized; just one of the stations has a library attached to it and a sports field on top. Nevertheless, the completion of the essential part of the scheme has contributed greatly to linking the barrio to the center of the city. The project's success has also shown that standard planning strategies that focus on traditional solutions such as simply inserting streets into the densely populated areas need to be rethought.

Architecture for the Other 90 Percent[19]

For some time now a few large organizations have devoted themselves to the task of resolving social conflict with the help of architecture. For example, together with UNESCO, the Union Internationale des Architectes (UIA) announced in advance of its world congress in Beijing in 1999 a public competition for "design ideas that could contribute to the eradication of poverty." There were 386 submissions that, after being juried, were exhibited in Beijing.[20] The proposals in the competition were never meant to be realized; instead, the idea was to generate concepts that would initiate dialogue and push the boundaries of what is possible. UN-Habitat, a division of the United Nations, works toward more humane urban development by means of presentations, conferences, and resolutions, and sponsors its own programs.[21] Other professional organizations focus on single aspects of humanitarian assistance, like teaching better building techniques or providing access to drinking water in remote areas.[22] One of the most successful organizations in this area is Architecture for Humanity, founded in 1999 in response to the war in Kosovo. It has taken on the task of promoting design and development services in places where they are urgently needed. In 2007 it launched the Open Architecture

Network, a Web site that helps to bring architects, designers, engineers, nonprofit organizations, political representatives, and others together in order to collaborate on projects and share expertise.[23]

These organizations largely respond directly to natural disasters, the consequences of war, and other humanitarian emergencies. They must react quickly to specific situations, and in most cases the architects' responses are by necessity ad hoc design efforts. This work is extremely important and, unfortunately, will likely be needed long into the future. But there is equally a need for institutions that are able to become familiar with regional needs and can work toward achieving sustainable improvements.

One influential organization that concentrates on long-term development is the Aga Khan Development Network, a group of agencies dedicated to improving the living conditions of the poor primarily in sub-Saharan Africa, Central and South Asia, and the Middle East. The Aga Khan Trust for Culture, for example, promotes building projects for impoverished segments of the population, but also places special emphasis on projects that respect regional traditions. Since 1977 the organization has called attention to the social implications of the profession with the Aga Khan Award for Architecture. (Kéré's school in Burkina Faso and Heringer's Handmade School in Bangladesh won the award in 2004 and 2007, respectively.)

Another important initiative, known as SEED (Social Economic Environmental Design), was founded in 2005. The aim was to develop a way to measure the social, economic, and environmental impact of building projects. The name recalls LEED (Leadership in Energy and Environmental Design), the "green" building certification system. Whereas LEED standards are designed to offer a clear definition of environmentally sustainable practices, SEED puts forward that sustainability equally refers to a project's social ramifications.

Communities can measure the social and economic impact of a project through an evaluation process that can result in a certification. While aesthetics and environmental issues play a role in this evaluation, the social impact of a design is the primary consideration. As the examples included here demonstrate, there is much to be gained when architects become responsive to the community. Their approaches must not be driven by preconceived political or architectural theories, but rather consist of responses to given realities. To increase the social relevance of architecture at the beginning of the twenty-first century, architects must no longer think of themselves simply as designers of buildings, but rather as moderators of change.

1   For recent data in the fight against poverty see The Millennium Development Goals Report by United Nations (2009), www.un.org/millenniumgoals/pdf.

2   According to Jean Dethier, there are about twenty different techniques of building with earth. Dethier, *Down to Earth: Adobe Architecture. An Old Idea, a New Future*, trans. Ruth Eaton (New York: Facts on File, 1983), p. 8.

3   Beth Hunter, "Rammed-Earth Houses: An American Vision in the New Deal," *Vulcan Historical Review* (University of Alabama at Birmingham) 13 (2009), pp. 85–97.

4   For Frank Lloyd Wright, see David Easton, *The Rammed Earth House* (White River Junction, VT: Chelsea Green Publishing Company, 1996), pp. 16–17. Le Corbusier published a small book, *Les Maisons "Murondin,"* on the techniques of rammed earth (Paris: Etienne Chiron, 1942).

5   For a discussion of the different techniques, see Ronald Rael, *Earth Architecture* (New York: Princeton Architectural Press, 2009). Rael discusses molded earth on p. 179.

6   Though the village was largely completed, ultimately the government did not force the inhabitants to move from their old village, and the project was abandoned.

In 2010 New Gourna was put on the World Monuments Fund's watch list. See http://www.wmf.org/project/new-gourna-village.

7 Italian architect Emilio Caravatti is another figure who has adopted the lessons of Fathy, above all with respect to reviving the technique of the Nubian vault. Now with his private foundation, Africabougou, in Mali, he promotes the use of traditional materials and sustainable approaches in building schools and hospitals, and helps to train craftsmen in such methods who can then apply their skills elsewhere. See "Public Buildings in the Mali Republic," *Domus* 915 (June 2008): 10–19.

8 Rael, *Earth Architecture*, pp. 126–29.

9 For example, the Kapelle der Versöhnung in Berlin (1990–2000) was the first building in Berlin using this material as a constructive element.

10 More and more specialists are offering their knowledge and know-how in these areas to developed and developing countries alike. Joe Dahmen, for example, at MIT, consults on rammed-earth projects around the globe. Earth Structures, a niche construction firm, uses earth-building techniques in industrial and commercial capacities, while CRATerre, at the University of Grenoble, France, concentrates on work in developing countries.

11 The volume *Expanding Architecture Design as Activism*, ed. Bryan Bell and Katie Wakeford (New York: Metropolis Books, 2008), contains a number of lectures given at the conferences and sums up new strategies about how design can become more relevant in global societies.

12 For the projects and history of Rural Studio, see Andrea Oppenheimer Dean and Timothy Hursley, *Rural Studio: Samuel Mockbee and an Architecture of Decency* (New York: Princeton Architectural Press, 2002), and the same authors' *Proceed and Be Bold: Rural Studio After Samuel Mockbee* (New York: Princeton Architectural Press, 2005).

13 For a brief history of UW BaSiC, see *Studio at Large: Architecture in Service of Global Communities*, ed. Sergio Palleroni (Seattle and London: University of Washington Press, 2004), p. ix.

14 The idea of an "incremental house" had in fact been proposed as early as 1931, in a competition sponsored by the city of Berlin. A group that included Walter Gropius, Hugo Häring, Egon Eiermann, and others worked up proposals for constructing single houses in stages, as owners could afford them. Some of these were executed and exhibited in the 1932 building exhibition *Sonne, Luft und Haus für Alle!*, in Berlin, but with the rise of Fascism and the architects going to exile the idea did not take root. The history of this exhibition, as well as some examples for later attempts to continue the concept, can be found in Anja Fröhlich, " 'Sonne, Luft und Haus für Alle!' – Das wachsende Haus. Ein Versuch zur Lösung der Wohnungsfrage unter besonderer Berücksichtigung der Rolle Martin Wagners" (PhD diss., Bauhaus-Universität Weimar, Germany, 2008).

15 "Learning from Tijuana," Teddy Cruz in conversation with Caleb Waldorf, *triplecanopy*, no. 7, http://www.canopycanopycanopy.com/7/learning_from_tijuana.

16 Though much has been written on the topic of slums and slum-upgrading, two very helpful overviews about the situation can be found in Eduardo Lopez Moreno and Rasna Warah, Urban and Slum Trends in the 21st Century, UN Chronicle, The State of the World's Cities Report 2006/2007; and Robert Neuwirth, *Shadow Cities: A Billion Squatters, a New Urban World* (New York: Routledge Taylor & Francis, 2006).

17 *The Favela-Bairro Project: Jorge Mario Jáuregui Architects*, ed. Rodolfo Machado (Cambridge, Mass.: Harvard University Graduate School of Design, 2003) is a brief description of this program published on the occasion of the sixth Veronica Rudge Green Prize in Urban Design, which was given to Jáuregui in 2000.

18 "Rio ist so etwas wie ein Zukunftslaboratorium," interview with Jorge Mario Jáuregui about the urbanization of favelas, in Elisabeth Blum and Peter Neitzke, eds., *FavelaMetropolis: Berichte und Projekte aus Rio de Janeiro und São Paulo* (Berlin: Birkhäuser, 2004), p. 77. (Original interview in German, translation from Jáuregui's Web site, http://www.jauregui.arq.br/entrevistas.html#04)

19 In 2007 the Cooper-Hewitt National Design Museum, New York, organized an influential exhibition titled *Design for the Other 90%* that presented innovative, accessible solutions to problems confronting the world's poorest populations. The exhibition was on view May 4–September 23, 2007, before traveling to four other locations. See http://other90.cooperhewitt.org.

20 See Jörg Seifert, "386 vergessene Ideen," *Archithese* 2 (2007): pp. 12–17.

21 The World Urban Forum 5, held in March 2010 in Rio de Janeiro, focused on the theme "The right to the city – bridging the urban divide."

22 For example, Architects Without Borders, Fondation Architectes de l'urgence, Engineers Without Borders, Architecture for People in Need, Habitat for Humanity, and Builders Without Borders.

23 In the book *Design Like You Give a Damn: Architectural Responses to Humanitarian Crises* (Los Angeles: Metropolis Books, 2006), the society presents a wide range of projects worldwide that address social needs.

METI—HANDMADE SCHOOL

Rudrapur, Bangladesh
2004–06

Anna Heringer

With more than one thousand inhabitants per square kilometer, Bangladesh is one of the most densely populated countries in the world. Roughly two-thirds of its people make their living from agriculture, yet a high birthrate means that the amount of arable land per capita is shrinking and the production of foodstuffs is becoming increasingly difficult. The dearth of land and extreme poverty are causing increasing numbers of the rural population to migrate to the cities. Concentrating the normally single-story dwellings in the country closer together and strengthening regional economies would help to alleviate some of the strains felt by rural communities, but initiatives aimed at addressing such issues are often hampered by local building traditions and the scarcity of income-producing employment in rural areas.

In 1997–98 Anna Heringer spent a year in Rudrapur, a village of roughly 1,500 inhabitants in the north of Bangladesh. She went there as a volunteer with Dipshikha, a local nongovernmental organization that works on development programs in such areas as education, health, income-generation support, and agriculture. She has subsequently returned to Rudrapur for several weeks each year. In 2002, as an architecture student at the University for Arts and Industrial Design in Linz, Austria, she undertook a comprehensive analysis of the village that she completed, together with three other students, over the course of six months. The goal of the study was to identify and document Rudrapur's civic and economic structure, beginning with making the first map of the village and then documenting the building types and materials and techniques they found. The biggest problem they identified is the scarcity of land for agriculture, which is the only source of income. Based on the insights she gained, as well as her knowledge of the lack of local educational opportunities, in 2004 Heringer decided to design a school for Rudrapur as her master's thesis, hoping that she could ultimately see her project realized. A seminar with Martin Rauch, a leading practitioner of earth architecture, convinced her it would be feasible to adopt traditional building materials in her design.

Heringer was aware that there was a tradition in Rudrapur of building with earth, but also knew

রুদ্রপুর

Master plan

that it was often badly executed: the walls were too thin, foundations were rough or nonexistent, roofs were inadequate. Further, builders in the country tend to consider the material primitive and unstable, and prefer to work with brick or concrete—both more expensive and energy-intensive ways to build. Based on the knowledge she gained from Rauch as well as her mentor, University of Arts and Industrial Design professor Roland Gnaiger, Heringer decided to use cob—clay, earth, sand, and straw mixed with water that is shaped by hand or trowel in layers and dried—with the hope of creating a new appreciation for this sustainable building material.

Dipshikha was already operating a school in the village, but in highly unsatisfactory spaces. It had drawn up preliminary plans for an expansion, but Heringer approached the organization and its subsidiary agency METI (Modern Education and Training Institute) about adopting her design. She demonstrated how her approach would offer the children brighter, better-ventilated spaces and explained the benefit of earth construction in giving children a healthier and more pleasant environment for learning. The organization also recognized the potential impact that building with earth could have for local workers and the village as a whole, and it eagerly accepted her proposal.

After nearly a year of planning and fund-raising, construction on the school began in September 2005. The two-story structure has three classrooms on the ground floor and two on the upper floor. The lower level is constructed of thick cob walls, which support a lightweight bamboo structure that in turn supports the corrugated metal roof. The two floors are connected by an open staircase. The exterior walls were left raw with the rough spade marks visible, while the interior walls were coated with a light-colored plaster. Caves carved out of the massive back wall provide hiding places where children can play or read. The upper story is a continuous space (the classrooms only separated by the stairs), closed off from the outside by wood framing filled with vertical strips of bamboo. The bamboo offers protection from the sun while still lending a light and airy feeling to the interiors, as well as offering views of the village. The rooms on both levels are cooled by cross-ventilation.

Eike Roswag, an architect from Berlin who assumed the job of construction manager, supervised the training of the local craftsmen. He also adapted the design to local conditions and developed details such as the joints for the bamboo. Aside from two craftsmen from Germany and several students from Linz, all the work was done by unskilled laborers from Rudrapur, with the idea that they would gain useful experience in cob construction. (The water buffalo employed in mixing the cob were the only additional help required.) A few essential improvements on local building traditions were introduced, namely the laying of a brick foundation and the introduction of a layer of plastic that serves as a moisture barrier between the ground and the earthen walls. Further, the walls were made thicker than in traditional buildings, and the addition of straw to the mixture offers more stability. The roofline was also extended beyond the walls to prevent them from being damaged by the heavy rains of the monsoon season.

Though taller than other structures in the village, the school's proportions were carefully calculated so as not to dominate its surroundings. Numerous windows are playfully scattered across the walls of the school. The deliberate use of color throughout also lends a cheery, inviting appearance. The doors on the ground floor were painted in different colors, and behind them hang vibrantly hued curtains. On the upper floor, lengths of locally produced cloth in bright colors brighten up the ceilings.

Heringer's initial design also envisioned a school garden, teachers' residences, and additional teaching spaces for older and adult students, elements that are slowly being realized. To date, a facility for electrical skills training has been completed, and the school will soon undertake the building of the garden. Several two-story model houses built of cob have also been erected for village families.

—AL

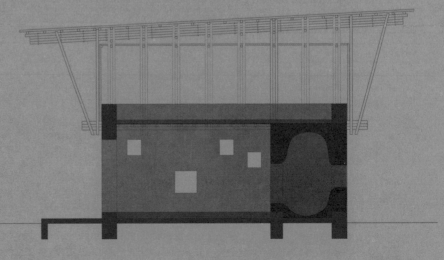

Section

ANNA HERINGER

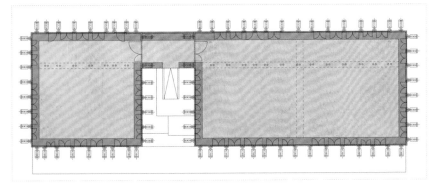

Upper-floor plan

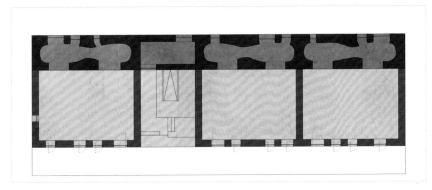

Ground-floor plan

South elevation   North elevation

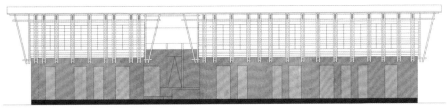

East elevation

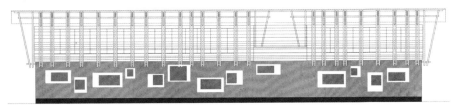

West elevation

Views of construction

ANNA HERINGER

METI—HANDMADE SCHOOL

ANNA HERINGER

METI—HANDMADE SCHOOL

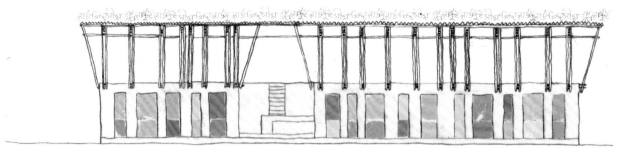

East elevation sketch

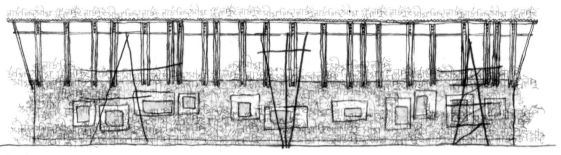

West elevation sketch

Following page
Top **Upper-floor classroom**
Bottom **Ground-floor cave**

PRIMARY SCHOOL

Gando, Burkina Faso
1999–2001

Diébédo Francis Kéré

Architect Diébédo Francis Kéré was born in 1965 in Gando, a village of some 2,500 inhabitants in the landlocked West African nation of Burkina Faso. The town lies about 125 miles (200 kilometers) from the capital of Ouagadougou. It is made up of a collection of circular farmsteads loosely scattered across the savanna and surrounded by agricultural land. The farmsteads are generally occupied by extended families and are still built in the traditional manner, with mud bricks and straw

roofs. Gando does not have electricity (only fifteen percent of the country is electrified), indoor plumbing, or even a paved street.

Burkina Faso ranks among the world's poorest countries, with nearly half of the population living below the poverty level. Its economy is based primarily on agriculture, but yields in its climate zone are subject to extreme fluctuations. Nearly seventy percent of the country's income comes from subsidies and foreign credits. Burkina Faso also has one of the highest illiteracy rates in the world; less than a third of its adult population is able to read and write. Though the government has made efforts to improve the education system, to a great extent the building of schools remains dependent on foreign aid, and therefore proceeds only sporadically. Another difficulty the country faces is the fact that, owing to the population's almost total dependence on agriculture, large numbers of children are put to work in the fields to ensure the survival of village communities and thus are not able to go to school.

In 1972 Kéré's parents sent him to school in Tenkodogo, the country's second largest city, about 8 ½ miles (13 kilometers) away. But when it turned out that the daily round-trip trek on foot was too exhausting for him, he was placed with relatives

Aerial view of Gando

when school was in session. After finishing grammar school in 1978, Kéré began an apprenticeship as

a carpenter, then in 1985 recei[ved a] scholarship to be trained as a teacher of woodworking in Germany. From 1990 to 1995 he attended an evening high school in Berlin, where he earned a diploma, then from 1995 to 2004 he studied architecture at Berlin's Technische Universität (TU). Since 2004 Kéré has taught at the TU, and in 2005 he established his own architecture office based in Berlin.

During his architecture studies, Kéré learned that the small primary school that had been built in his hometown the year after he left was in disrepair. After first sending money for upkeep, he soon realized that this was of little long-term benefit. Some of his fellow students in Berlin convinced him that he should use his knowledge to go to his hometown and build a better school himself. In 1998 he set up an organization called School Building Blocks for Gando, with the goal of building a completely new school. He also began a dialogue with the villagers, soliciting their input and ensuring that when the time came the community would help to construct the school. Kéré hoped to use what he had learned in Germany about ecological building techniques to provide a model for future schools that were both sustainable and more suited to local needs.

Kéré's school consists of three detached rectangular classrooms placed in a row. The intervening roofed spaces can be used for recesses or outdoor instruction. Despite large class sizes—traditionally fifty pupils per teacher—the interior spaces retain a generous feel, in part thanks to the relatively high ceilings. Light falling in from the sides, filtered through hinged metal louvers, takes on a warm tint due to the reddish adobe walls. Abundant air circulation helps maintain pleasant inside temperatures on even the hottest days. To aid in this Kéré decided to rest each building's corrugated metal roof atop a light structure of distinctive girders, rather than place it directly on top of the supporting walls, which results in heat radiating directly into the room below. Below the girders he placed a concrete frame to hold a ceiling of thin clay tiles fitted into metal supports. The ceiling serves as both insulation and an acoustic barrier below the metal roof. The roof also projects beyond the walls below, keeping both rain and the midday sun away from the masonry, and the elongated structures' east-west orientation further limits excessive heating of each building's long side walls by the sun.

One of the major problems Kéré saw with traditional school construction concerned the actual building materials that were used: most of the country's schools had been built with concrete blocks, which are relatively expensive and require a great deal of energy to produce. For his project the architect turned to the government agency LOCOMAT, which encourages the use of local building materials. With its support Kéré taught the villagers how to make adobe bricks using a few improvements that add tremendously to the quality and life span of the finished product. Traditionally, the bricks are formed by hand in wood frames and dried. Kéré introduced a simple machine, powered by nothing but two people, that makes more stable, uniform bricks by forming them in a mold and then pressing them. This, together with a small amount of cement added to the adobe (roughly six percent), makes the bricks stronger and more uniform. The result is straighter walls and a stronger surface that better weathers the elements.

It was important that the school's structural elements could all be assembled by hand by workers on-site, both because it was not possible to bring heavy machinery to the village and because the training of workers was a critical component of the project. For the girders Kéré designed a simple, triangular shape that could be created by local craftsmen. The roof was also fashioned on-site, bent into the curved shape directly on the supporting truss. The building of the school was truly a community endeavor, with villagers supplying most of the labor. Some of the workers who trained in the production of clay bricks and

the construction of the school have since found work as skilled laborers at other building sites.

Despite nine years of intensive use, the school shows little sign of aging. Compared to others in the region, some of more recent date, the Gando model stands out as a striking example of how building techniques that are sustainable as well as appropriate to local conditions can produce architecture of far superior quality. More importantly, the facilities provide the children of Gando with a place where they can acquire the basic skills that will benefit both them and their families. Since the school opened, interest has been extremely high. Applications have far outpaced available spots, and even children from nomadic families who were previously not sent to school are now enrolled. The number of teachers has risen from three to nine. Thanks in part to the broad recognition of the project's success, Kéré has been able to gradually expand his concept. In 2008, given the high attendance figures, the architect built a fourth classroom following virtually the same concept. He has also completed houses for the teachers, and has plans for an adjacent library and a women's center.

—AL

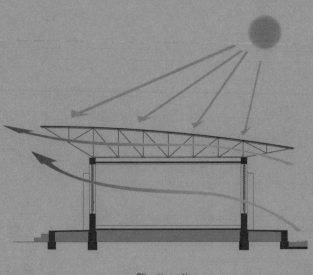

Climatic section

DIÉBÉDO FRANCIS KÉRÉ

West elevation

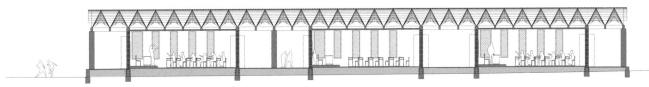

Longitudinal section

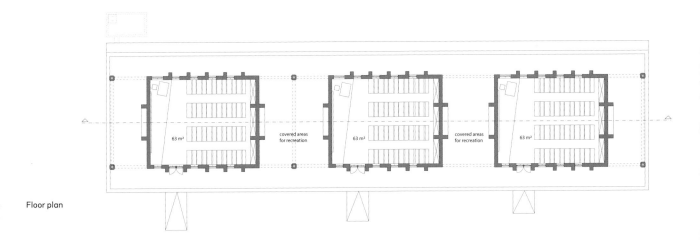

Floor plan

63 m²   covered areas for recreation   63 m²   covered areas for recreation   63 m²

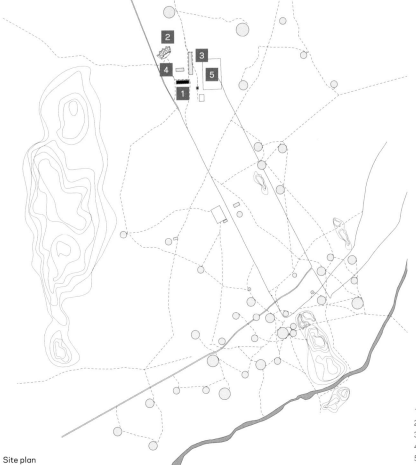

Site plan

1   School building
2   Teachers' housing
3   School extension
4   Old existing school
5   Sports field

DIÉBÉDO FRANCIS KÉRÉ

PRIMARY SCHOOL

DIÉBÉDO FRANCIS KÉRÉ

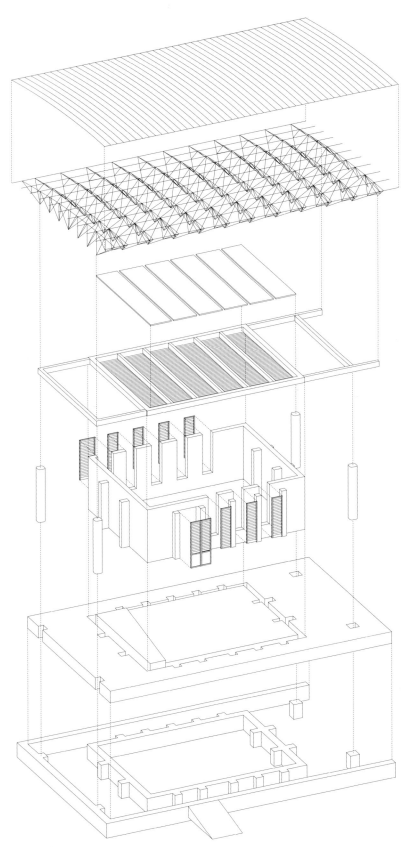

Exploded axonometric

Top **Roof construction**
Bottom **Detail of roof**

PRIMARY SCHOOL

HOUSING FOR THE FISHERMEN OF TYRE

Tyre, Lebanon
1998-2008

Hashim Sarkis A.L.U.D.

Tyre, Lebanon, is an ancient coastal city located 50 miles (80 kilometers) south of Beirut that has been burdened by a turbulent recent history. A weak economy and decades of tumult have debilitated the maritime city. Owing to its location as an entry into the country's Hezbollah stronghold and a frequent combat zone, Tyre has long struggled to maintain a viable infrastructure amid seemingly constant chaos.

While the conditions in Tyre are difficult for all residents, the area's fishermen—many of whom live on as little as fifteen dollars a day in the high season—have been particularly hard hit. Long-standing conflict with Israel has directly impacted their livelihood by preventing them from deep-sea fishing in the Mediterranean, leaving small and unprofitable yields. Further, in 1984, during the Lebanese Civil War, the city was added to the UNESCO World Heritage List thanks to its rich archaeological past and Roman ruins. Though this distinction brought hopes for preservation and immunity from attack, it also brought restrictions within the newly protected coastal area, including strict regulations on new building along the coastline, where the fishermen and their families have traditionally lived. The result has perpetuated overcrowded, damp, and ultimately unsanitary living conditions.

Housing for the Fishermen of Tyre is an eighty-four-unit complex built on a former radish field a few miles inland from the ancient city harbor. Built on one of the few larger parcels in Abbassiyeh, an area peppered by disorganized, ad hoc postwar development and subdivisions, the complex is the result of a decadelong collaboration between the local organization Al Baqaa Housing Cooperative, the Association for Development of Rural Areas in South Lebanon (ADR), and Lebanese architect Hashim Sarkis, whose practice and teaching have long been focused on architecture in the Islamic world. In 1998 the fishermen formed Al Baqaa, persuading the city's Greek Orthodox archdiocese to donate the 1.75-acre (.7-hectare) parcel of land on the agricultural outskirts of Tyre. With three thousand dollars from each family and financial support from local and international nongovernmental

Map of Tyre with housing complex at upper right

organizations, Al Baqaa and Sarkis were able to work together to create the necessary housing.

The concrete complex is a composite of nine residential blocks, each with a separate entrance. It is fortified by a rigid outside edge that defines the perimeter between the site and the surrounding urban disorder; the building turns in onto itself like a rectilinear nautilus, creating a protected interior courtyard. This shared space allows residents to gather and forge a sense of community. Paved and landscaped areas within the courtyard create distinct microclimates and encourage cross-ventilation in the hot summer months. Local trees such as olive, orange, and ficus allude to the site's agricultural past and create an oasislike environment.

Small passageways and two main vehicular access points are incised into the larger form, generating arteries for circulation throughout. Sarkis also designed networks of stairs that are open to the elements, increasing air circulation and natural light. The result is connection with the outside while privileging a sense of enclosure. Balconies, stair profiles, patios, and entryways are extruded, while other areas of the facades recede. This three-dimensionality creates a dynamic massing and lends the project a sense of the visual diversity and collectivity of a neighborhood. Some of the protrusions also afford shade from the heat.

Early on, Sarkis proposed that the complex consist of three different styles of apartment blocks, each with a unique arrangement of three different apartment typologies. Al Baqaa was initially skeptical of the idea of the differing plans, wanting all of the apartments to have the same layout. By using study models, drawings, and other pedagogical tools, however, Sarkis was able to demonstrate how offering each unit a balance of indoor and private outdoor space would compensate for inevitable inequalities in overall location and view. Every apartment includes some outdoor space: lower duplexes, on the ground and first floors of the building, have private gardens; one-story flats that face the interior road have a minimum of two balconies; and upper duplexes are afforded roof access. Each apartment is roughly 925 square feet (86 square meters), with about half as much in additional outside space.

Sarkis worked directly with Al Baqaa to manage the project's tight budget. He had originally planned to add abstracted geometric stenciling over stucco to the exterior of the buildings. Because of budget limitations, however, he and the project contractor chose to paint the entire complex. After an extensive series of facade color studies, the resulting scheme assigns cooler colors (blues and grays) to the exterior, warmer ones (yellows and oranges) to the interior, and a delineated bleed of the two at each intersecting elevation. Color is exaggerated where there is no sun, within the balconies and stair halls, in a playful experiment with light and shadow.

Over the course of the project, the plans were steadily thwarted, both because of dwindling funds and national turmoil. The February 2005 assassination of former Prime Minister Rafic Hariri and the 2006 Lebanese-Israeli War added untold months onto the project. Both Al Baqaa and Sarkis, however, demonstrated admirable tenacity, and saw the project through. Housing for the Fishermen of Tyre, among the architect's very earliest commissions, has also been a catalyst for other collaborations with Lebanese civil organizations. Synthesizing architecture, landscape, and urban planning, Sarkis's complete ethnographic approach to architecture communicates the transformative power of design to offset and even improve chaotic conditions and mitigate marginalization. In patiently translating his clients' needs into built form, Sarkis has added order and logic to the area, while maintaining a sense of inclusion and community for the displaced fishermen.

—MW

View of complex

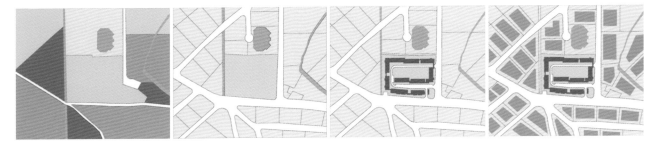

Diagram of site development

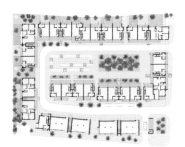

Ground floor

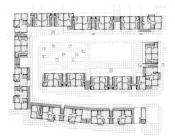

Floor 2

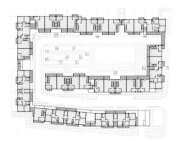

Floor 3

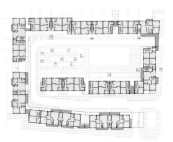

Floor 4

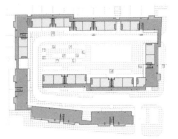

Floor 5

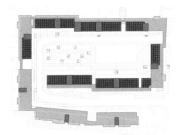

Roof

Top View of courtyard
Bottom View of southeast corner

HASHIM SARKIS A.L.U.D.

2-duplex / 4-simplex
apartment block

4-duplex
apartment block

4-simplex
apartment block

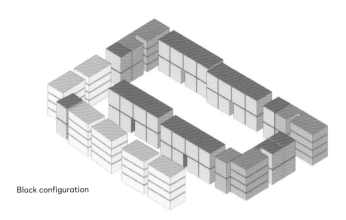

Block configuration

Open space allocation per unit

Unit distribution diagram

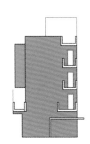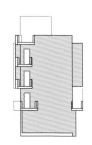

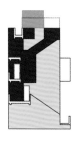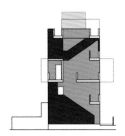

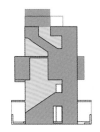

Top Color studies, Building I
Bottom Side elevations

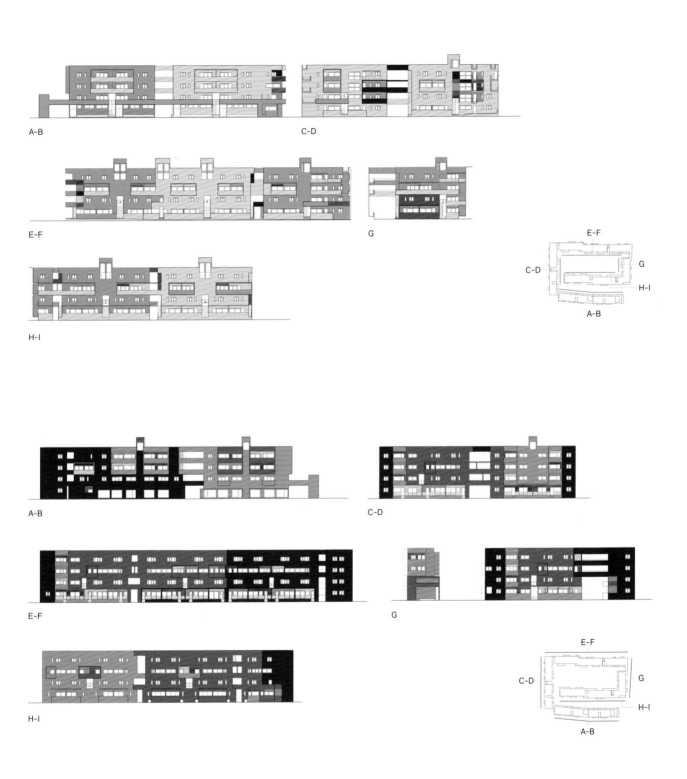

A-B

C-D

E-F

G

H-I

A-B

C-D

E-F

G

H-I

E-F
C-D
G
H-I
A-B

E-F
C-D
G
H-I
A-B

Top Interior elevations
Bottom Exterior elevations

HASHIM SARKIS A.L.U.D.

HOUSING FOR THE FISHERMEN OF TYRE

RED LOCATION MUSEUM OF STRUGGLE

Port Elizabeth, South Africa
1998–2005

Noero Wolff Architects

The Red Location Museum of Struggle serves as an important hub for one of the oldest townships in South Africa. Red Location, which is a part of New Brighton, in Port Elizabeth, was set up in 1902 at the end of the Second Boer War. After 1948 Red Location—the name derives from the rust color of the ubiquitous corrugated iron shacks—developed into one of the centers of the antiapartheid movement; a number of its leaders, including Govan Mbeki and Raymond Mhlaba, were born there or lived there for a time, and some of the historic protest actions originated there. In 1986 the apartheid government tried to demolish the township and resettle its inhabitants, hoping to break up this hotbed of dissent. Massive demonstrations led to the abandonment of this plan, but the repression of the populace only increased, with raids and violent actions on the part of the military police.

Following the abolition of apartheid, in 1994, plans for a number of museums dedicated to the history of the brutal regime and those who fought against it were begun around the country. The Port Elizabeth city government decided to build a museum—places to which blacks had once been denied entry as visitors—memorializing the apartheid era right in the township of Red Location, thereby making the historic site of resistance an integral part of the experience. It announced a national competition for plans, and the winning design was submitted by the firm Noero Wolff Architects, established in 1985 by Jo Noero. After studying architecture at the University of Newcastle upon Tyne in Britain, Noero decided to return to South Africa to apply his skills in his home country. Thanks to his background as an active member of the antiapartheid movement since 1979, he had come into contact with Archbishop Desmond Tutu, who named him the architect for the Transvaal diocese in 1982. Through this position he received a number of commissions in the nongovernmental sector, which allowed Noero to actively use his profession to assist the poor and oppressed black community. Beginning in the 1980s he realized several low-income housing projects in addition to the building of churches.

From the outset, a main issue in the planning of the museum was the future acceptance of the institution within its neighborhood. To this day, Red Location's community association, which played an important role in overcoming apartheid, remains highly suspicious of outside attempts to introduce structural changes. For this reason a community-based project committee met weekly throughout construction to ensure that the concerns of the community were being met. It stipulated that a third of the unskilled laborers were to come from the museum's immediate environs, so that they might receive training on the project. In order to ensure that a large number of community members could gain experience, workers would spend three months on the job before new workers would take their place. Though this raised costs and extended construction time, the city felt it was a worthwhile trade-off both for the skills it imparted to local residents and for the neighborhood's acceptance of the facility.

The exterior of the museum recalls the industrial buildings in the surrounding township. Simple concrete pillars, unplastered brick walls, and sawtooth roofs give the

Axonometric site plan

---

exterior a functional appearance, and ordinary building materials such as brick and concrete were used throughout the design. According to Noero, "The language of the new buildings is utilitarian and industrial, and it is hoped that this will act as a connection to a proud union past and seek to remember the labor of those people who gave up their lives for the struggle." A broad entrance portico with a timber pergola serves as a transition space between the surrounding shacks and the museum entrance. This open area is an inviting gathering place for the people of the neighborhood. There is also an outdoor movie theater that can seat up to 2,500 people.

The design of the interior is as simple and basic as the exterior. The pillars that hold the roof, as well as the floor and the dividing walls, are all constructed of polished concrete. The roof structure is open to the interior, adding to the impression of an industrial factory space. The defining elements of the museum are the so-called memory boxes, twelve display spaces nearly 50 feet (15 meters) tall and 20 feet (6 meters) square and sheathed in rusty corrugated iron. These versatile exhibition spaces recall the large, painted trunks in which black migratory workers would carry their belongings and mementos from home. The rotating content displayed in these spaces may include documentation of personal histories or installations dedicated to various themes such as local music or political protests and their leaders. The memory boxes do not present a linear historical narrative; rather, visitors are encouraged to explore these spaces on their own. In this way the galleries become more a laboratory in which the museumgoer must actively participate in weaving together the various stories of Red Location—experiences that also resonate in the community just outside.

The long-term goal is to use the museum as an anchor in a new museum precinct, which will ultimately include a library, an art center, a market hall, and sports facilities in addition to the apartheid museum. Subsequent phases of Noero Wolff's master plan, such as the art museum and the archive, are already under construction. As visitors start to come in greater numbers, over time this influx will help to improve the economy of the surrounding area. Though it is understood that such improvements will take years—perhaps even decades—to realize their full impact, more than two hundred jobs have already been created throughout the construction, and nearly half of these have translated into permanent positions. Currently, about seventy people work in the museum, or as tour guides or in other small businesses that cater to tourists.

—AL

Top Aerial view of site, 2000
Bottom Aerial view of site, 2007

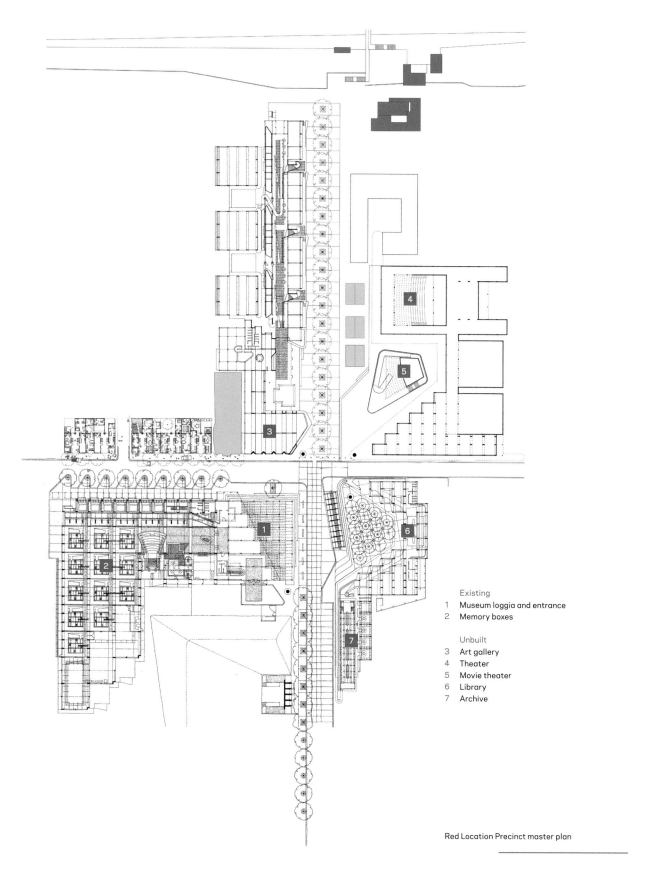

Existing
1 Museum loggia and entrance
2 Memory boxes

Unbuilt
3 Art gallery
4 Theater
5 Movie theater
6 Library
7 Archive

Red Location Precinct master plan

View from museum entrance loggia

_____

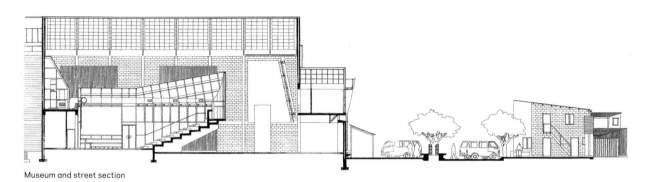

Museum and street section

South elevation

East elevation

Section

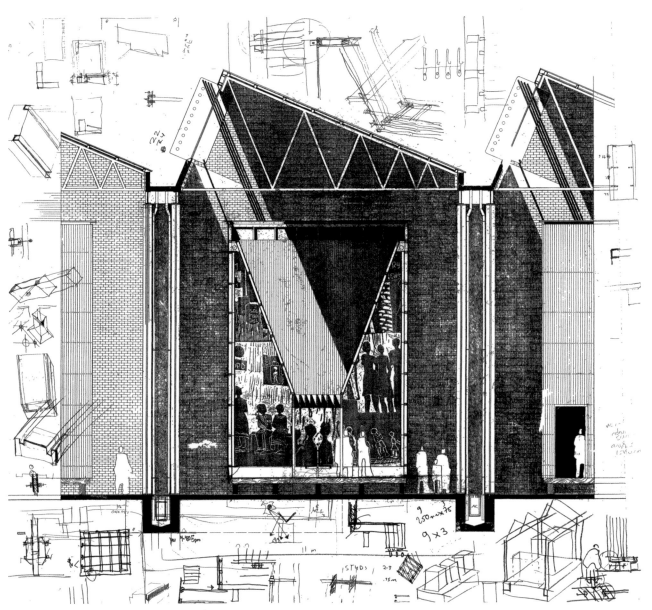

Memory Box working section

RED LOCATION MUSEUM OF STRUGGLE

Museum interiors

NOERO WOLFF ARCHITECTS

INNER-CITY ARTS

Los Angeles, California
1993–2008

Michael Maltzan
Architecture

Inner-City Arts, located in an impoverished Los Angeles neighborhood just a short drive from the city's cultural and financial center, offers a creative refuge to at-risk and disadvantaged children who may not otherwise have access to the arts. Here, young people have the opportunity to encounter such pursuits as ceramics, painting, sculpture, drama,

Site plan

and animation. Founders Bob Bates, an artist and educator, and Irwin Jaeger, an entrepreneur, hoped to address the lack of arts classes in nearby public schools through a partnership not only with administrators but also the

local community. Their proposal was partly in response to Proposition 13, passed in the late 1970s, which called for severe tax caps that led to, among other things, virtually eliminating arts education from many of the state's public schools. Two decades after its founding, Inner-City Arts offers classes taught by professional artists to approximately 10,000 elementary-, middle-, and high-school-aged children every year, at no cost to the participants, and is heralded as being among the most effective arts-education organizations in the country.

After several years of conducting classes in trailers and other temporary spaces, ICA set out to establish a permanent home. The organization teamed up with local architect Michael Maltzan and his newly formed firm in 1993 to retrofit an abandoned auto body shop in LA's dangerous Skid Row neighborhood. The renovation, completed with Marmol Radziner and Associates, entailed stripping the 8,000-square-foot (750-square-meter) garage to its structural elements in order to create a cavernous, multipurpose space for classrooms, performances, and administrative

offices. Maltzan aimed to invite in as much light as possible through three existing garage doors and skylights. The resulting space is a simple and highly adaptable backdrop for the various activities of the school. Maltzan also designed a sculptural tower, which houses ceramics facilities and a kiln, and a storage shed just north of the garage windows.

In 1995, a few years after the completion of this first phase, ICA purchased an old warehouse building and lot just north of the auto body shop, an acquisition that allowed the school to expand into nearly a whole city block. In response Maltzan developed a master plan that would accommodate more students at the continuously growing institution. Due to the need to raise funds, the plan was realized during two different building periods, beginning in 2002. In 2005, the school expanded into the warehouse on the northwest corner of the site, nearly tripling their space by adding more visual arts and animation studios, a gallery, and a kitchen. The addition of rooftop parking on this new building was vital for the security of the faculty and administration. The most recent phase, which added studio and administrative spaces, a resource library, a second ceramics tower, a black-box theater, and connecting passageways, was completed in 2008.

The finished campus employs a restrained and refined architectural language, with simple geometric massing and clean white walls defining the center both inside and out. Flexible interior and exterior spaces make for an intimate yet airy arena for kids and endow the organization with an adaptable space. One of the biggest challenges was to connect the aggregate campus with its context while retaining a sense of enclosure. Careful cutouts and setbacks along the northeast and northwest corners create interactive sightlines that link the school to its surroundings and make the overall massing less imposing. Low walls in places further open the school to its site, fostering a strong relationship with the neighborhood. Because of security reasons, however, these exterior surfaces are seldom punched through with windows. The campus's ceramics towers, visible from points in the neighborhood, serve as beacons for the school. Landscape architect Nancy Goslee Power designed a main courtyard that is a comfortable and inviting environment to gather, play, and explore within a neighborhood whose outdoor space is scarce and often unsafe. The landscape design augments a sense of protection and lends interior interest by using a combination of local plant life, from palm trees to succulents. In painting the exterior stucco walls a bright white, the organization communicates its commitment to continued maintenance and upkeep. After fifteen years of planning and building, ICA has a one-acre campus that feels open and expansive yet tranquil and protected, and most importantly provides a safe and playful place for the Skid Row community.

—MW

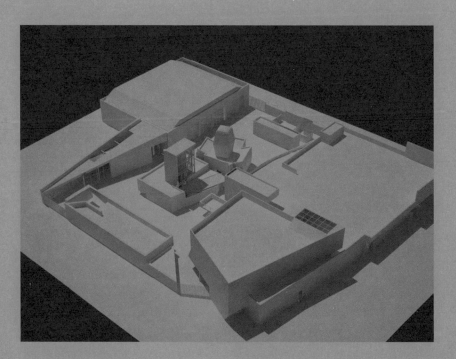

Rendering of the site

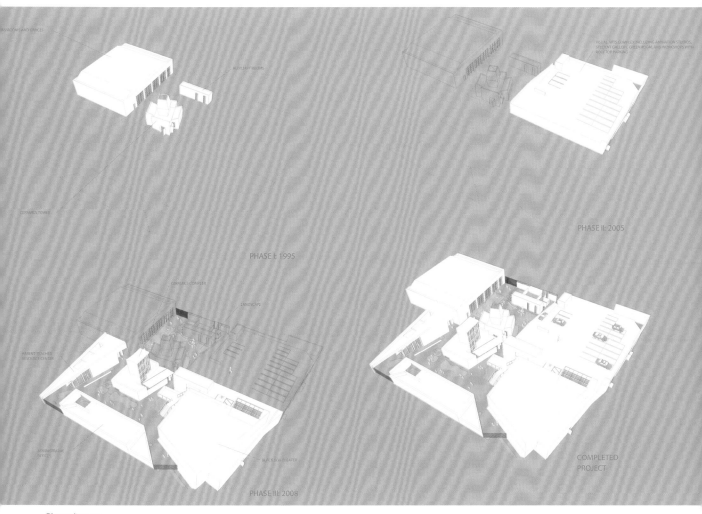

CLASSROOMS AND OFFICES

AUXILLARY ROOMS

VISUAL ARTS COMPLEX INCLUDING ANIMATION STUDIOS, STUDENT GALLERY, GREEN ROOM, AND WORKSHOPS WITH ROOFTOP PARKING

CERAMICS TOWER

PHASE II: 2005

PHASE I: 1995

CERAMICS COMPLEX

LANDSCAPE

PARENT TEACHER RESOURCE CENTER

ADMINISTRATION OFFICE

BLACK BOX THEATER

COMPLETED PROJECT

PHASE III: 2008

Phase diagram

INNER-CITY ARTS

MICHAEL MALTZAN ARCHITECTURE

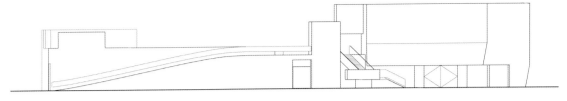

North elevation

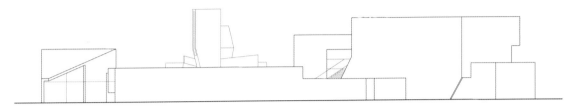

East elevation

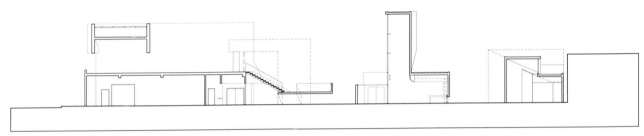

North-south section

Proposed exterior signage

Top **View of northeast corner**
Bottom **View of courtyard**

MICHAEL MALTZAN ARCHITECTURE

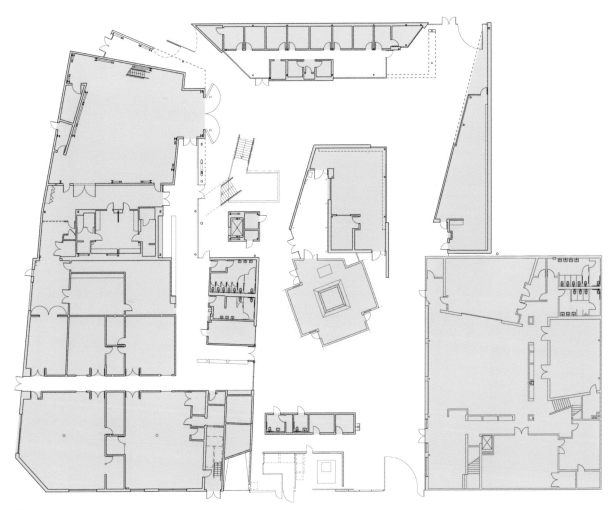

Floor plan

Interior of ceramics tower

$20K HOUSE VIII (DAVE'S HOUSE)

Newbern, Alabama
2009

Rural Studio, Auburn University

Founded in 1993 by Samuel Mockbee and D.K. Ruth, Rural Studio is a satellite school for undergraduate architecture students of Alabama's Auburn University. The mission of Rural Studio, located in Newbern, an impoverished town of some three hundred people 150 miles (240 kilometers) west of Auburn, is to teach students design and building skills as well as the coincident ethical and social responsibilities of the profession—to educate the "citizen architect." To date, Rural Studio has completed about 120 private and public projects, including houses, community centers, chapels, and sports facilities, across three adjacent Alabama counties. The success of these initiatives is testament to the school's long-term commitment to Newbern. Over the last decade Rural Studio, which has been under the directorship of British-born Andrew Freear since Mockbee's death in 2001, has slowly shifted away from Mockbee's interest in poetic, single-family homes toward broader community interventions.

The $20K House, a research project started in 2005 that aims to address the dearth of decent, affordable housing in western Alabama, represents another step in this direction. Each year since its inception, a new group of students has worked together to design an inexpensive yet dignified house that could eventually be used as an easily replicated model for low-income rural housing. The starting point for the project is the Rural Housing Service's Section 502 Direct Loan, a federal program that allows qualified residents—those without sufficient credit to qualify for a standard loan and with income only from public assistance or Social Security—to borrow money (up to $124,000 in 2010) to buy a house. Of the 6,427 households in Hale County, forty percent are eligible to apply for this loan (around thirty percent of all residents live below the poverty line), the majority of whom are elderly or disabled. With few options for housing, many residents find themselves living in trailers, whose value and quality depreciate precipitously.

With this in mind, Rural Studio decided their goal was to design a house that would be available for the tiny sum of $20,000, which would keep the resident's monthly payment to about $100. If one such house could be built every three weeks (another directive of the project), roughly sixteen houses could be built each year. In addition to creating a transformative effect on the area's housing, the project also aims to generate a microeconomy by purchasing materials locally and using area contractors and workers to construct the houses, further benefiting income-starved Hale County.

So far nine designs have been drafted (one a year except for 2007–08, when four designs were developed in tandem) and then built at the end of each term by the students and their instructors. It goes without saying that the strict budget forces an economy of decisions, and some versions have come closer than others to meeting the project's goals in terms of budget and construction time. Later years have benefited from evaluating both the successes and shortcomings of earlier iterations. The best designs are sculpturally simple, each detail fastidiously considered, their reduced grammar and rigorous simplicity minimizing cost and accelerating construction time.

The 2008–09 team has come closest to creating a viable prototype. Rather than starting anew, the team, Charity Bulgrien, Ian Cook, and Obi Elechi, developed a variant of Frank's House, designed in 2005–06, itself a succinct interpretation of the shotgun typology. Through systematic observation and conversations with Frank, who has lived in the house since its completion, the team honed in on several areas they deemed problematic: first, Frank's house has two porches, the bigger of which is in the back and remains largely unused; second, the interior of Frank's house is completely open, with just curtains separating the joint bedroom and bathroom from the rest of the house; third, the exterior corrugated tin is considered shack-like and impermanent by local residents.

The resulting form of version VIII, built for local resident David Thornton, is an almost anonymous architecture, rooted in the everyday.

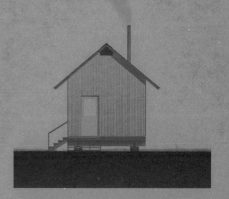

Rear elevation

Modest and spare, the house is distilled to the most elemental and irreducible details. Set on an elevated pier foundation for ease of construction, the house is an extruded box with a generous front porch, capped by an open gable roof. The box, which measures just over 600 square feet (56 square meters), is mostly unarticulated, interrupted only by an interior core that neatly encloses the bathroom and separates the bedroom from an open living room and kitchen with a small connecting wall. High ceilings, four windows, and front and back doors make for a comfortable, well-ventilated space. The white pine screened-in porch—the epicenter of residential life in the summer months—is a social extension of the living room. The house is clad in white corrugated tin—an inexpensive finish that recalls traditional white siding but is still durable and low-maintenance.

The team divided the $20,000 budget into roughly $12,000 for materials and $8,000 for labor, and the house was constructed in stops and starts over a three-month period, using only simple tools. As with other Rural Studio projects, construction comes at the end of a nearly yearlong period of design development, research, one-to-one mock-ups, sketches, client presentations, and studio and on-site critiques. In the case of Dave's House, the students built on campus a one-to-one mock-up of the front porch to better understand its massing and construction details. The porch was then deconstructed, edited, and eventually rebuilt on-site.

With a regenerating pool of students, university funding, and a rich building history, all in relative isolation, Rural Studio is an ideal laboratory. Using the same time-tested methods in operation since 1993—careful research, dedication to the local community, continued stewardship of past projects—the school is slowly, tenaciously setting the framework for a new paradigm of low-income rural housing. With this project, the architect (here in training), often an arbiter between a client's wishes and practicality, design and budget, is seeding a partnership between residents and local agency. Dave's House was the first $20K House to be built by a local contractor in real-time conditions, as the first of several steps toward formalizing a truly repeatable model. More

recently, the 2009–10 team has tested a version that includes plans for potential expansion. Looking further into the future, Freear envisions developing a catalogue of a few different typologies—perhaps even a family home—that could be adapted to different needs and made available wherever rural housing loans are obtainable.

—MW

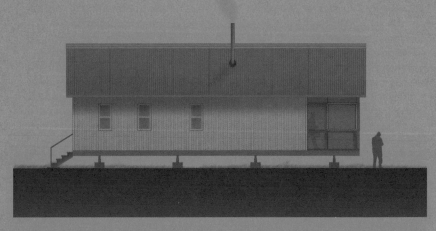

Side elevation

I

II

III

IV

V

VI

VII

VIII

$20K Houses I–VIII

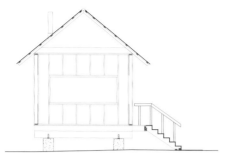

Front elevation

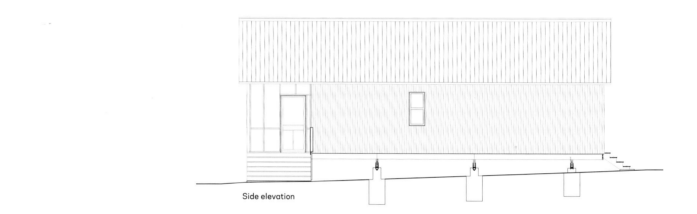

Side elevation

Rear elevation

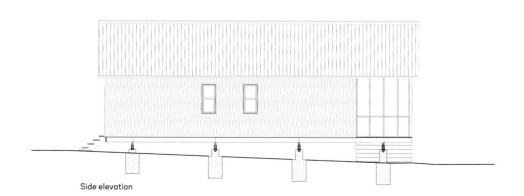

Side elevation

Porch mock-up

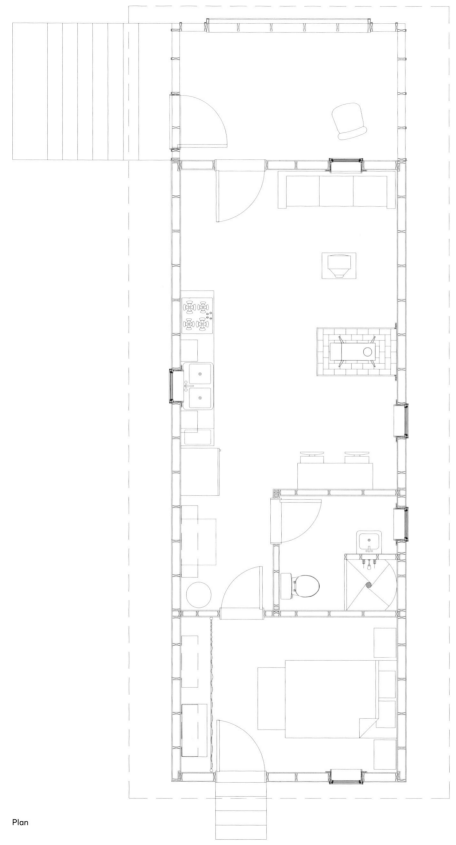

Plan

$20K HOUSE VIII (DAVE'S HOUSE)

Views of construction

$20K HOUSE VIII (DAVE'S HOUSE)

$20K HOUSE VIII (DAVE'S HOUSE)

QUINTA MONROY HOUSING

Iquique, Chile
2003-05

Elemental

Chilean architect Alejandro Aravena turned his attention to low-income, high-density social housing in 2000, while teaching at the Harvard Graduate School of Design (GSD). It was there that he met Andrés Iacobelli, a Chilean engineer studying public policy and a kindred spirit also interested in addressing social inequity through built form. Over the next several years, their collaboration evolved into Elemental, a unique for-profit partnership between Aravena and Iacobelli, which has since expanded to include large Chilean oil company Copec and Pontificia Universidad Católica de Chile, Aravena's alma mater. According to Elemental, Chile will spend around $10 billion over the next fifteen years to address its low-income housing deficit. In response, the group's team of architects, engineers, social workers, and contractors, unconventionally aligned with an oil company, is working to reassess social housing as an entrepreneurial opportunity rather than an expense that must be borne by the state.

In 2003, Elemental—a self-proclaimed "do tank"—at its inception also linked with the GSD, was commissioned by the government's Barrio Chile program to create housing for a community of nearly one hundred low-income households on a half-hectare (1.25-acre) site in central Iquique, a desert city of 200,000 people in northern Chile. For several decades this community had been informally and illegally occupying the highly valued downtown parcel.

Following the program, the tiny sum of $7,500 per unit was to cover the cost of land, infrastructure, and building for each family. Further, the government encouraged Elemental to find a solution that would not displace the community from their existing site.

Given the limitations of the per-family sum—Aravena estimated it could yield a maximum of 30 built square meters (320 square feet)—the architects decided the best approach would be to only partially build each house. Their solution was a building type that could both be inhabited right away and allow for significant changes over time. This dynamic approach would allow each family to quickly receive the benefit of a high-quality shelter, which is then expanded over time. The team decided on a variation of the traditional row house in which each unit consists of one built segment flanked by an equal-size void. The goal is for the facades of the dentiled arrangement to recede as each family completes the massing of its unit, adding swatches of color, texture, and vitality. Rather than one family inhabiting a single three-story building, the interiors are divided into ground-floor units and upper-floor duplexes. The larger settlement is grouped into dense clusters of twenty to thirty houses, creating communal courtyards and generating organized social space outside the confines of each dwelling.

Beginning in 2004, ninety-three basic reinforced-concrete units stabilized for seismic durability were built over a period of nine months. These spartan shells provided the barest of basics: roughed-out plumbing but no fittings for the kitchen or bathroom, an access stair, openings for doorways, and other integral parts of each unit. Once this modular, load-bearing outline was completed, residents were able to move in and begin finishing out their spaces. Within months after moving into the complex, they started to expand into the framework, using the architects' carefully planned and roughed-out openings as guides. Over time the units were vividly filled

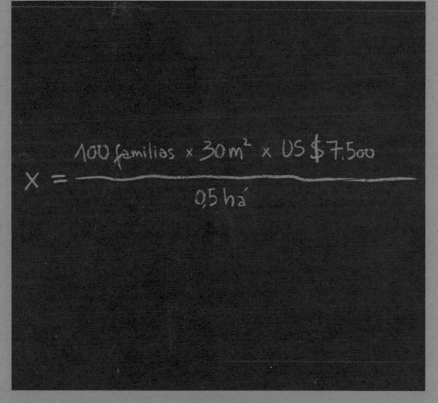

$$X = \frac{100 \ \text{familias} \times 30\,m^2 \times US\$7.500}{0,5\,ha}$$

out and filled in piecemeal with walls, windows, fittings, and decorative flourishes, adding to each house a sense of individuality. The hope is that such a model, in which customization and appreciation is achieved through gradual investment and sweat equity, will lead to a more lasting solution for social housing.

The success of the project relied on dialogue and a cooperative spirit between Elemental and the residents, with everyone contributing to the fabric of the neighborhood. Residents were given guidance on how to create stable, long-lasting expansions. Elemental used a variety of pedagogical tools, including simple blocks, drawings, and even life-size plan layouts, to help facilitate the transition. Paper models of individual units helped residents plan for and envision their house and the completed neighborhood. Residents in smaller cluster workshops developed hand-colored drawings, initiating discourse about neighborhood aesthetics, regulations, and possible standardization of expansion finishes, like window treatments and facade colors. To help facilitate this work, the architects deliberately drafted voids that would accommodate simple, standard-size construction materials in order to make adding on as simple as possible. Completed units more than doubled in size to roughly 70 square meters (750 square feet).

In developing this model on land in central Iquique, several times more expensive than land used for standard low-cost housing in Chile, Elemental rejects the marginalization that often relegates low-income housing to the outskirts of a city. This repositioning also has the potential to limit urban sprawl as well as areas of concentrated negativity sometimes associated with social housing. Elemental's site-specific solution, which came out of highly restrictive fiscal and political conditions, has since been adapted and refined elsewhere. Later iterations complete more of the structure in the initial phase and require somewhat less construction from residents (for example, Monterrey, in Mexico, completed in 2010, provides a full roof for all of the upper units). The team has erected well over one thousand expandable units in Latin America and beyond, and has another thousand in development. It is also currently working with Brad Pitt's foundation Make It Right on a housing prototype for New Orleans. Elemental's brick-and-mortar critique of the status quo demonstrates that social housing can be addressed through adaptive design, without sacrificing individuality or access.

—MW

Left Demonstration of footprint
Right Community planning workshop

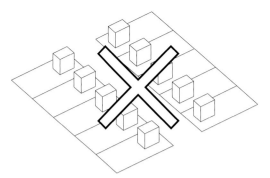

1 house = 1 lot

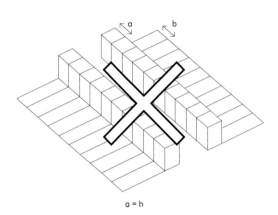

a = b

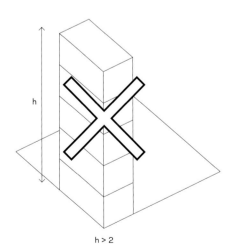

h > 2

Rejected typologies

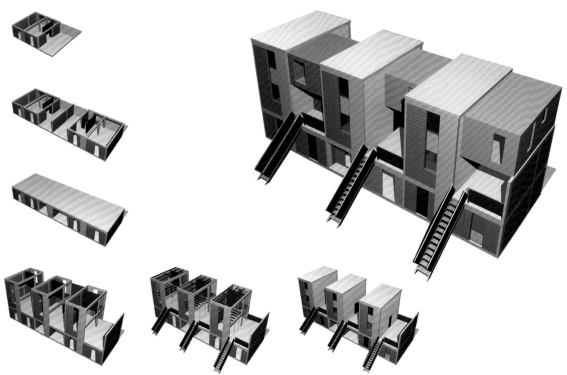

Construction phases

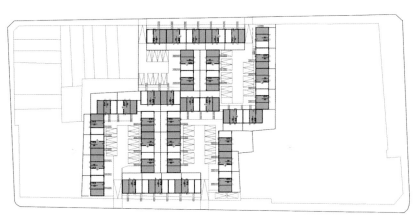

Site plan

QUINTA MONROY HOUSING

Top View of Iquique
Bottom Units before expansion

QUINTA MONROY HOUSING

QUINTA MONROY HOUSING

ELEMENTAL

CASA FAMILIAR: LIVING ROOMS AT THE BORDER AND SENIOR HOUSING WITH CHILDCARE

San Ysidro, California
2001–present

Estudio Teddy Cruz

San Diego–Tijuana border illustration

Like the visionary architects of the 1960s and '70s, Guatemala-born, San Diego–based architect Teddy Cruz prefers not to build new buildings. However, instead of the wild, quixotic concepts of his forebears, Cruz proposes affecting existing environments through shifts in established infrastructure and policy. Estudio Teddy Cruz, established in 1993, takes a collaborative, sociopolitical approach to design. Together with his firm, Cruz is intimately engaged with the highly permeable boundary between the United States and Mexico at the San Diego–Tijuana border, and his understanding of the movement of materials, people, and ideas in both directions dictates much of his practice.

In 2001 Cruz began collaborating with community-based nongovernmental organization Casa Familiar to develop a pilot project for San Ysidro, located just across the border from Tijuana. Casa Familiar has been working since 1968 to help San Ysidro's almost exclusively Latino population, providing advocacy and programming in such areas as immigration services, education, and job placement as well as spearheading community-based development efforts. According to Casa Familiar, around two-thirds of San Ysidro households are multifamily, and the median income in this area is sixty percent less than the rest of San Diego County.

Though the impetus of the project was to provide affordable housing, the team sought to develop a concept that would also stimulate the neighborhood more holistically. In studying the area, Cruz found a wide variety of ad hoc uses of land—garages and outbuildings that have been converted into bedrooms and extensions of living space, and commercial, cultural, and religious entities—that have infiltrated the formerly homogenous suburban area. The architect and Casa Familiar sought to invent a system that would resonate with the dense, multiuse, and often illegal development that has been common in the area. The first and perhaps most significant step in this process was to identify and legalize zoning rules appropriate to the density and income levels present in San Ysidro. This work stemmed from parcel-by-parcel observations of so-called nonconforming uses within residential lots. It was also informed by monthly workshops, known as San Ysidro Sin Limites, that helped the organization and Cruz to discuss and challenge conceptions of density, community, communal space, and financing with the local residents. This decade-long undertaking has culminated in designs for two projects on abandoned or underutilized parcels: Living Rooms at the Border and Senior Housing with Childcare, two small-scale, affordable-housing developments with integrated multiuse indoor and outdoor spaces, which are expected to break ground in summer 2011.

For Living Rooms at the Border, Cruz has developed a flexible, multiuse complex. At the center of the site is an abandoned white stucco church, dating from 1927, which will be retrofitted and expanded to house Casa Familiar offices and a community center. Flanking this are four parallel buildings that contain both housing and adaptable community space. Ten rental apartments, ranging in size from studio to four-bedroom, are organized in the two outermost buildings, one for small families and one for larger ones. Units for the smaller families are set upon a concrete frame and share several community kitchens. In and around this simple, linear structure is where Casa Familiar will be able orchestrate its many programs, accommodating

Photo-collage showing proposed housing, gardens, and church

a wide variety of social, cultural, and commercial functions. The larger apartments are housed in a set of simple two-story structures linked by a sawtooth roof on the other edge of the lot. Two other nonresidential buildings beside the church provide yet more multipurpose space. Vegetable gardens will help to promote healthy eating, while a rainwater-collecting system will make the garden and landscaping self-sufficient. Photovoltaic cells will be added to many of the roofs in order to return energy to the grid. All told, the nearly 15,500-square-foot (almost 1,500-square-meter) site comprises a dynamic fabric of socially and ecologically sustainable components.

Senior Housing with Childcare is another multipurpose affordable-housing project around the corner from Living Rooms at the Border, to which it is connected by pedestrian promenades. Thirteen new two-bedroom rental apartments, a childcare center, and a community kitchen have been designed for a generation of older immigrants who are in custody of their grandchildren. The apartments are to be organized in seven narrow, rectilinear buildings placed parallel to one another; the eighth building will house the childcare center. Where each of the buildings' rooflines thrust upward will be a lofted second bedroom. Attached to one edge of each building will be an open-air shed that provides multiuse community space. As with Living Rooms at the Border, private and community garden spaces,

also featuring an integrated system for rainwater collection and solar panels, will complement this new construction. Between each of the units will be a small strip of ground that both allows for circulation and accommodates small gardens.

Through his radically pragmatic architecture, Cruz seeks not only to understand the fabric of the immigrant neighborhood but to institutionalize it. By facilitating the collaboration between Casa Familiar, local government, residents, and others, such as developers and investors, the architect is able to mediate bottom-up and top-down intervention. Because his process allows him to design a complete plan unique to the needs and conditions of this border town, Cruz aims to have a lasting impact on the community of San Ysidro.

—MW

This page
Top Graphic showing Tijuana's mixed-use density infiltrating Southern California
Middle Parcel-by-parcel investigation of land use in San Ysidro
Bottom Street views of existing land use

Following spread
Development of zoning policy for San Ysidro

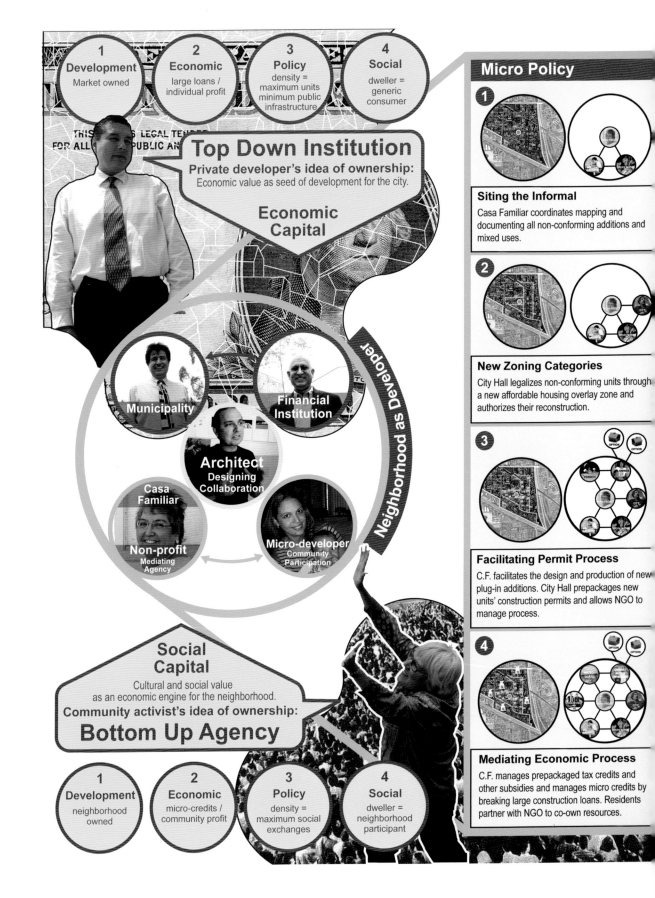

1 Development
Market owned

2 Economic
large loans / individual profit

3 Policy
density = maximum units minimum public infrastructure

4 Social
dweller = generic consumer

Top Down Institution
Private developer's idea of ownership:
Economic value as seed of development for the city.

Economic Capital

THIS IS LEGAL TENDER
FOR ALL PUBLIC AND

Municipality

Financial Institution

Architect
Designing Collaboration

Casa Familiar
Non-profit
Mediating Agency

Micro-developer
Community Participation

Neighborhood as Developer

Social Capital
Cultural and social value
as an economic engine for the neighborhood.
Community activist's idea of ownership:
Bottom Up Agency

1 Development
neighborhood owned

2 Economic
micro-credits / community profit

3 Policy
density = maximum social exchanges

4 Social
dweller = neighborhood participant

Micro Policy

1

Siting the Informal
Casa Familiar coordinates mapping and documenting all non-conforming additions and mixed uses.

2

New Zoning Categories
City Hall legalizes non-conforming units through a new affordable housing overlay zone and authorizes their reconstruction.

3

Facilitating Permit Process
C.F. facilitates the design and production of new plug-in additions. City Hall prepackages new units' construction permits and allows NGO to manage process.

4

Mediating Economic Process
C.F. manages prepackaged tax credits and other subsidies and manages micro credits by breaking large construction loans. Residents partner with NGO to co-own resources.

Plugging Support Systems Into Housing

roof texture framing social program

shared kitchen as social corridor

Senior Housing with Childcare

pocket garden with neighborhood kitchen

Youth

Sweat Equity

Casa Familiar

Arts and Culture

Community Based Non-Profit

Education

Seniors

Livingrooms at the Border

units + social service infrastructure

non-profit offices

community center

workshops

playground

market

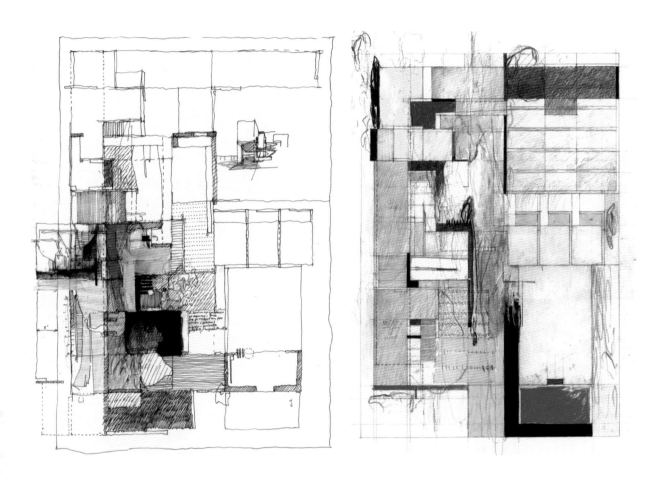

This page
Site sketches for Living Rooms at the Border

Facing page
Top Concept collage using Donald Judd's *15 Untitled Works in Concrete* (1980-84)
Bottom Renderings for Living Rooms at the Border

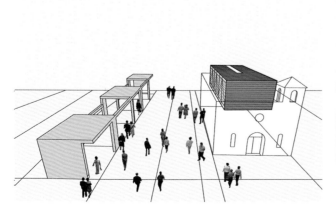

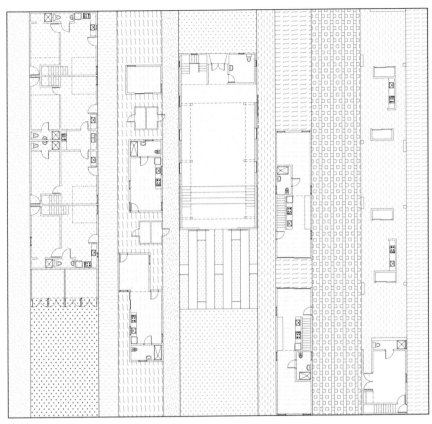

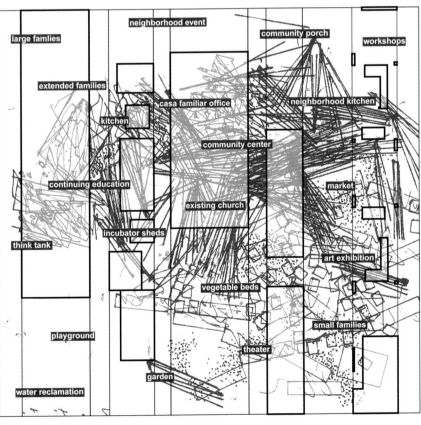

large famlies

neighborhood event

community porch

workshops

extended families

casa familiar office

neighborhood kitchen

kitchen

community center

continuing education

market

existing church

incubator sheds

art exhibition

think tank

vegetable beds

small families

playground

theater

garden

water reclamation

CASA FAMILIAR: LIVING ROOMS AT THE BORDER AND SENIOR HOUSING WITH CHILDCARE

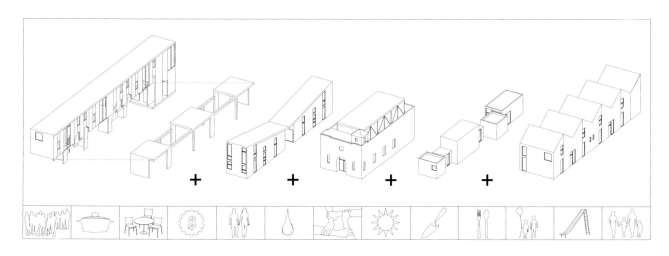

Social Service Infrastructure	Casa Familiar Programs		Informal Uses / Time Scenarios	Unit / Collective-Kitchens / Co-Ownership
	Tues 3:30 PM	ARTS WORKSHOPS		
	FARMER'S MARKET	Sun 9:30 AM		
	Sat 7:30 PM	QUINCEAÑERA		
	COLLECTIVE KITCHEN	Wed 6:00 PM		
	Mon 10:30 AM	CATERING LEASE		
	PUBLIC SYMPOSIUM	Sat 4:00 PM		
	7:30 PM	GARDEN ORIENTATION		
	GALLERY SHOW	Fri 8:00 PM		
	Sat 10:00 PM	BLOCK PARTY		

Facing page
Top Static plan for Living Rooms at the Border
Bottom Dynamic plan for Living Rooms at
the Border, layered over Barry Le Va's drawing
Three Activities (1968)

This page
Top Typologies included in Living Rooms at
the Border
Bottom Various applications of multiuse frame
over time

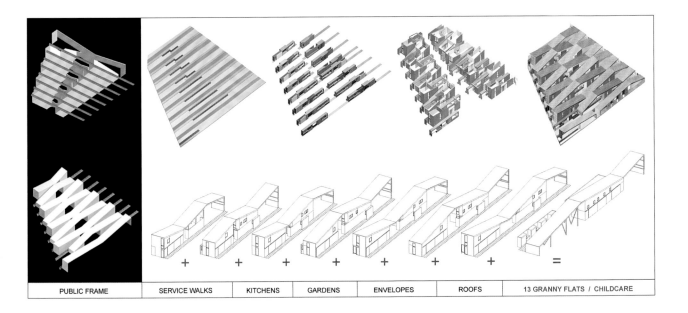

PUBLIC FRAME	SERVICE WALKS	KITCHENS	GARDENS	ENVELOPES	ROOFS	13 GRANNY FLATS / CHILDCARE

Composition diagram for Senior Housing
with Childcare

TRANS- FORMATION OF TOUR BOIS-LE- PRÊTRE

Paris, France
2006–11

Frédéric Druot,
Anne Lacaton, and
Jean Philippe Vassal

The modernist housing development has long been the subject of criticism. In particular, low-income, high-rise apartments blocks, generally clustered closely together, have been accused of being anonymous, monofunctional

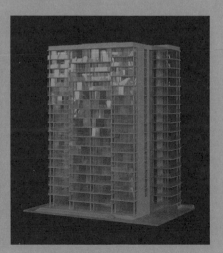

containers in which inhabitants are isolated from one another. The lack of communal space, shopping facilities, and cultural offerings have been seen as a failure of the concept itself. The demolition of the Pruitt-Igoe housing complex in St. Louis, Missouri, in 1972 confirmed

to many of the harshest critics that the model was fatally flawed. Charles Jencks even proclaimed that event to signal the end of modernist architecture.

The outskirts of Paris are filled with housing developments built in the 1960s and '70s whose very architecture has been blamed for contributing to the social problems that have arisen in and around them. In the Zone urbaine sensible (ZUS)— a term that refers to an area with large housing complexes now receiving special funds for redevelopment— unemployment is twice as high as the national average, and among young people it is even higher. In the wake of violent and prolonged rioting in the fall of 2005 in a number of poorer suburbs around Paris, politicians and others renewed calls for the demolition of such developments, hoping to create a tabula rasa on which to experiment with new concepts. Yet simply removing these structures without addressing the underlying reasons for their failure would only mask the social and economic problems faced by residents. Further, replacement housing comes with its own drawbacks, including

Models of towers before (left) and after (right) transformation

the wholesale dismantling of established communities.

Architects Frédéric Druot, Anne Lacaton, and Jean Philippe Vassal are

among those who reject the calls for demolition, favoring instead to retrofit existing structures. Through their work, they aim to demonstrate that adapting and upgrading is both more economical and ecologically sound than tearing down and building anew. In 2005 the three won a competition sponsored by the Office public d'aménagement et de construction de Paris (OPAC) to remodel a public residential high-rise in northern Paris by showing that their proposal would result in significant cost savings. This tower, which dates from 1961, was designed by Raymond Lopez and was built with prefabricated concrete components. (A nearly identical project by the same architect was built for the Interbau development in Berlin in 1957 and is now a protected landmark.) Though partners Lacaton and Vassal had completed conversions for single-family houses, for Bois-le-Prêtre they collaborated with Druot to implement the approach on a larger scale.

The Paris structure is sixteen stories tall and contains ninety-six apartments. The architects looked to make improvements to private as well as shared spaces. Based on previous research as well as interviews with a large number of building residents, the three decided to focus on expanding living spaces and increasing natural light in each apartment. Their proposal calls for the addition of a floor slab that would increase the footprint of each apartment by roughly fifteen percent, and a new exterior structure—a kind of shell that would completely envelop the existing building and break up the monotony of the former facade. (In contrast, apartments made available to renters displaced by demolition can be up to fifteen percent smaller than the ones destroyed.) Building out would allow the removal of the formerly outermost walls in order to create a new balcony in each unit. The new exterior, comprised of floor-to-ceiling glazing, provides the building's insulation.

Their plan calls for a number of improvements to the interior spaces as well. After studying the existing apartment layouts, the team developed a series of alternative and more individualized floor plans. For example, a former two-room apartment could become a large studio, or a former three-room apartment could become a four-room apartment. The plan also activates underused spaces on the lowest floors by creating common spaces, including a lounge and a movie theater. Two new elevators provide direct access to all floors of the building. The architects also looked to improve the entry lobby, both by making it accessible from the ground level instead of a staircase, and by modifying it to include views onto an interior garden. Construction on the project began in October 2009 and is expected to be completed by mid-2011. The work is being done in two parallel phases. As the prefabricated, modular facade structure takes shape, the interior floor plans are being modified and new openings are being created in the old exterior walls. By adapting existing structures to present-day housing needs, Druot, Lacaton, and Vassal are giving the eternally criticized residential high-rises of modernism new life.

—AL

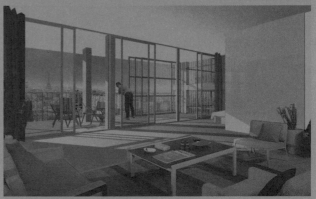

Views of apartment before (top) and after (bottom) transformation

Photomontage of expansion strategy

FRÉDÉRIC DRUOT, ANNE LACATON AND JEAN PHILIPPE VASSAL

Before

Transformation

After

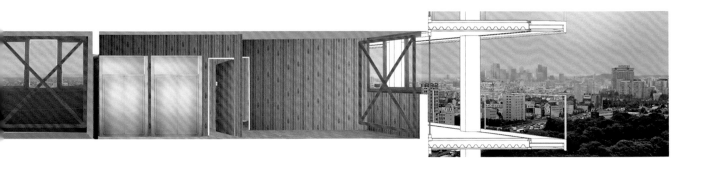

Typical floor

FRÉDÉRIC DRUOT, ANNE LACATON AND JEAN PHILIPPE VASSAL

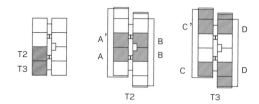

T2 before

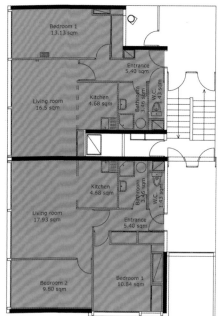

T3 before

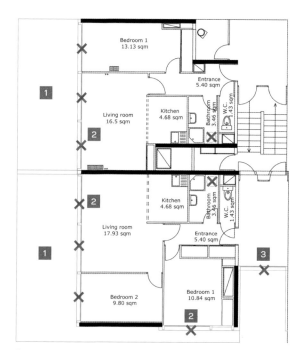

Opening intervention

1   Extension of floor slab
2   Removal of facade
3   Removal of facade for
     installation of new elevator
4   Removal of partitions
5   Reclamation of utility room
6   Addition of partitions

Proposal for lines A and A'
T2 with extension of 4 sq. m remains as T2

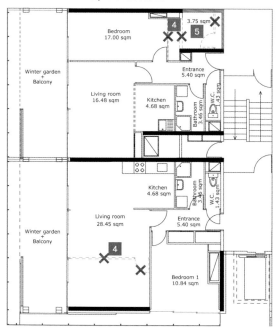

Proposal for lines B and B'
T2 without extension is transformed into T1bis

Proposal for line C
T3 without extension is transformed into new T2

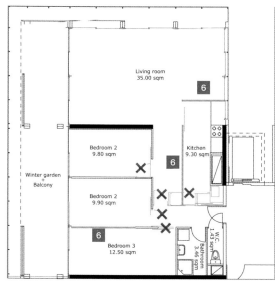

Proposal for lines C' and D
T3 with extension of 36 sq. m is transformed into new T4

Proposal for line D'
T3 with extension of 18 sq. m is transformed into new T3

FRÉDÉRIC DRUOT, ANNE LACATON AND JEAN PHILIPPE VASSAL

View of existing tower

TRANSFORMATION OF TOUR BOIS-LE-PRÊTRE

Rendering of completed transformation

FRÉDÉRIC DRUOT, ANNE LACATON AND JEAN PHILIPPE VASSAL

Diagrams of occupancy by unit type

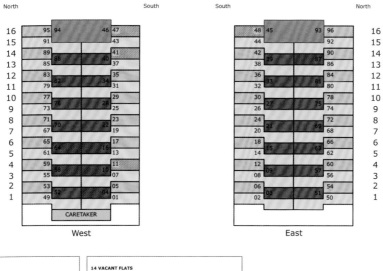

North   South   South   North

West   East

	Vacant	
	T5/6	32
	T3 (angle)	32
	T2(duplex R+16)	4
	T2(centre) 6/2	28
	T4 caretaker flat	1

14 VACANT FLATS
. 6 T2(centre)
. 4 T3 (angle)

After transformation
Redistribution of occupancy by unit type

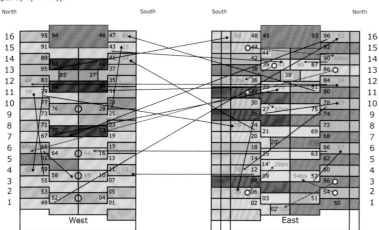

North   South   South   North

West   East

	VACANT	
	F7 - 3 (n° of flats) / 1 (n° of vacant flats)	
	F6 - 8	
	F5 (or old T5/6) - 17 / 2	
	F4 - 12 / 2	
	F3 - 13 / 1	
	F2 (or old t3, angle) - 17 / 1	
	T2 (duplex 17th floor) - 4	
	T2 (centre) - 6 / 2	
	F1bis (or old T2, centre, east) - 17 / 5	
	studio - 4 / 3	

○→	de-cohabitation
○	regrouping of two flats
49 → 49	internal movement
49 →	other possibilities

**This proposal takes into account
the following hypothesis :**
. sliding of n°20 and n°02, 2 strips to the south
. sliding of n°86, 1 strips to the north
. sliding of n°38, 1 strips to the south
. sliding of n°85, 2 strips to the north
. sliding of n°37, 2 strips to the south
. F4, n°52 + n°04, n°76 + n°28 possible for the caretaker

14 vacant flats :
. 3 studios
. 4 F1bis
. 2 T2 centre
. 2 F4
. 1 F7

MANGUIN-HO'S COMPLEX

Rio de Janeiro, Brazil
2005–10

Jorge Mario Jáuregui/ Metrópolis Projectos Urbanos

The Manguinhos district, in the north of Rio de Janiero, is a large urban area that is home to some ten favelas with roughly 28,000 residents. This troubled area stands adjacent to a major access route to Rio's urban center, and is criss-crossed by several main avenues, a river, a number of canals, and a rail line. It is also home to industrial plants, research complexes, and commerce. Like many of the city's favelas, those in Manguinhos suffer from a lack of public space and community facilities. Because of its extremely high crime rate, which often flares up in gang conflict and shootouts between the drug mafia and the police, one of the main thoroughfares, Rua Leopoldo Bulhões, has been dubbed "Death Avenue."

In 2005 Rio's city government asked architect Jorge Mario Jáuregui, along with his firm Metrópolis Projectos Urbanos, to undertake an urban-planning study of Manguinhos. Jáuregui set out to compile a comprehensive inventory of the district's social, economic, urban, and ecological features. He was selected for this project in part because of his long-term involvement in the Favela-Bairro Program, also in Rio, a slum-upgrading project that began in 1993. For that initiative, the architect designed a series of small interventions, such as daycare centers, sports facilities,

and communal laundries. Similarly, based on his findings in Manguinhos, Jáuregui developed a number of interconnected proposals for improvement, including the creation of a new community center, containing a library, a school, a health clinic, and an office providing legal advice next to a newly created train station.

Roughly twenty percent of the population of Rio proper, or some one million inhabitants, lives in the more than five hundred favelas scattered around the metropolis. Though many of these favelas have been in existence for a hundred years, their explosive growth—which surpasses that of the planned parts of the city—and the rising criminality within them have in recent decades forced politicians to actively address the problems often associated with them. One of the biggest challenges is to connect the favelas with the other parts of the

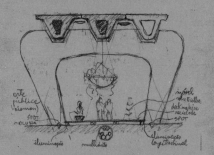

city. Most informal settlements do not benefit from public amenities such as water lines and sewer service, or have access to public transportation systems, health facilities, or parks. The incremental legalization of dwellings, which gives residents the ability to own their residences rather

than live in legal limbo, is also vital to stablizing these areas.

At the heart of Jáuregui's master plan was the idea of elevating a mile and a half section (2.4 kilometers) of the rail line adjacent to Rua Leopoldo Bulhões and creating a long public park beneath it. It was a notion inspired by Rio's Parque do Flamengo, designed by Roberto Burle Marx in 1961 to be a place for relaxation, leisure pursuits, sports, and cultural events—a "democratic

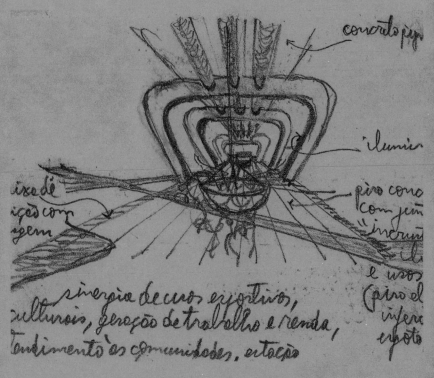

Preliminary sketches

space"—as well as by the Rambla in Barcelona, Spain. By raising the rail line, Jáuregui hopes to overcome a formerly insurmountable physical and psychological barrier between

Manguinhos and the rest of the city—and also to create a new public amenity. Once completed, the park will function as a central meeting place for the various parts of the sprawling district. The neighboring favelas, which tend to close in on themselves, will open onto the park. Amenities such as athletic fields, and bicycle paths will also be included.

Jáuregui began by conducting interviews and hearings with the district's inhabitants and representatives so as to better understand their immediate concerns as well as their long-term requirements. He also strove to include area residents in every phase of the design, from the initial planning to bringing in observers during the various construction stages. Particularly important to Jáuregui was limiting the number of people who had to be resettled due to the construction. Although a number of dwellings adjacent to the train line had to be torn down, the architect ensured that substitute housing was available on time, thereby creating greater trust in the entire project.

Due to political contraints, the city initially shelved the 2005 study. Three years later, however, it was taken up by the state of Rio de Janeiro, which assimilated it into the state-funded Development Acceleration Program. As with other upgrading projects for the city that are being planned in conjunction with Brazil's hosting of the 2014 FIFA World Cup, the project took on a new level of urgency. Although Jáuregui's original project was designed to be completed within twenty years and in a number of four-year segments, it was decided to realize all of it in a mere two years. Construction began in 2008 and completion is set for September 2010.

—AL

Aerial views of project site

JORGE MARIO JÁUREGUI / METRÓPOLIS PROJECTOS URBANOS

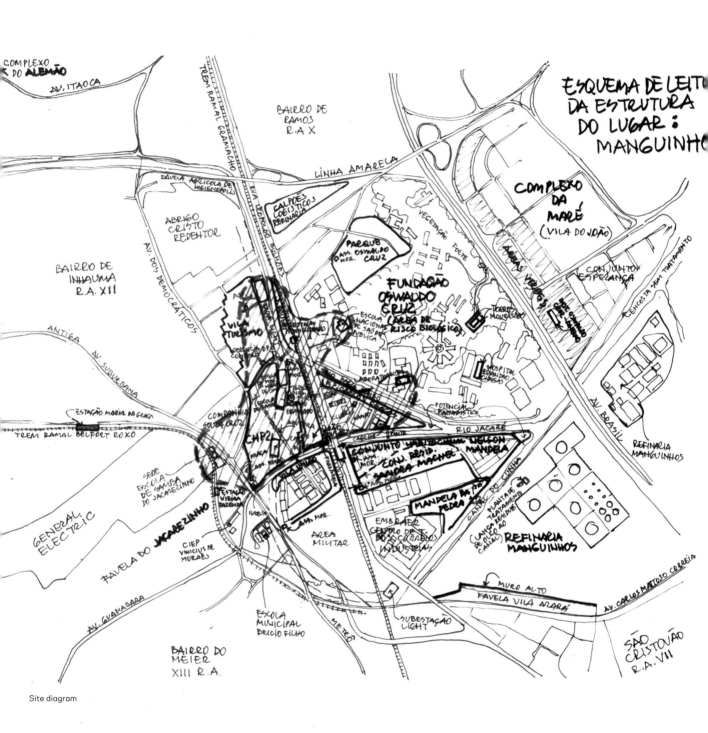

ESQUEMA DE LEIT
DA ESTRUTURA
DO LUGAR:
MANGUINHO

COMPLEXO
DA
MARÉ
(VILA DO JOÃO)

COMPLEXO
DO ALEMÃO

AV. ITAOCA

BAIRRO DE
RAMOS
R.A X

LINHA AMARELA

FAVELA AGRICOLA DE
HIGIENOPOLI

GALPÕES
LOGISTICOS
REFINARIA

ABRIGO
CRISTO
REDENTOR

PARQUE
ASS. OSWALDO
MOR. CRUZ

VEGETAÇÃO
FORTE

CONJUNTO
ESPERANÇA

ENCOSTA SEM TRATAMENTO

BAIRRO DE
INHAUMA
R.A. XII

FUNDAÇÃO
OSWALDO
CRUZ
(AREA DE
RISCO BIOLOGICO)

TORRE
MONGASCO

ANTIGA

AV. SUBURBANA

ESCOLA
NACIONAL
DE SAUDE
PUBLICA

HOSPITAL
EVANDRO
CHAGAS

AV. BRASIL

ESTAÇÃO MARIA DA GRAÇA

POTENCIAL
PAISAGISTICO

REFINARIA
MANGUINHOS

TREM RAMAL BELFORT ROXO

COMPANHIA
SOUZA CRUZ

RIO JACARÉ

SEDE
ESCOLA
DE SAMBA
DO JACAREZINHO

CHP2

CONJUNTO
MANDELA

CONJ. RESID.
SAMORA MACHEL

NELSON

GENERAL
ELECTRIC

MANDELA DA
PEDRA

CANAL DO CUNHA

PLANTA DE
TRATAMENTO

FAVELA DO JACAREZINHO

CIEP
VINICIUS DE
MORAES

ESTAÇÃO
VIEIRA
FAZENDA

EMBRAER
CENTRO DE T.
BOMBARDIO
INDUSTRIAS

LANÇA FALHAS
SE OLEO NO
CANAL?

REFINARIA
MANGUINHOS

AREA
MILITAR

AV. GUANABARA

ESCOLA
MUNICIPAL
BRICIO FILHO

METRÔ

SUBESTAÇÃO
LIGHT

MURO ALTO

FAVELA VILA ARARÁ

AV. CARLOS MATTOSO CORREIA

SÃO
CRISTOVÃO
R.A. VII

BAIRRO DO
MEIER
XIII R.A.

Site diagram

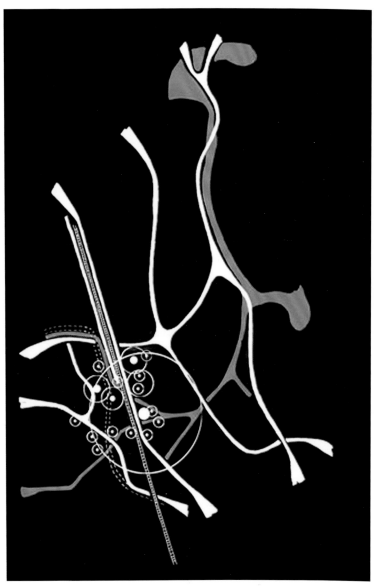

Ideogram of project site

General plan of intervention area

Rendering of Parque Manguinhos

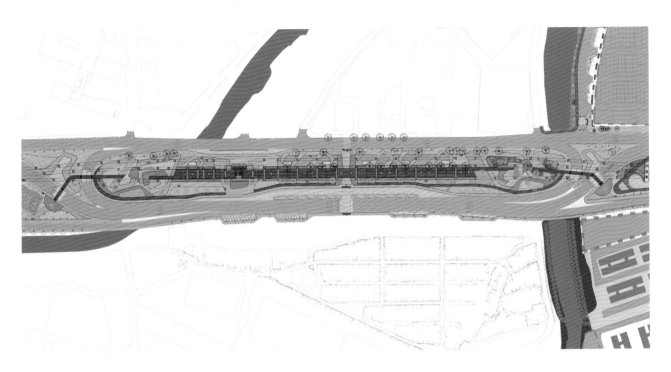

Top Plan of Parque Manguinhos
Bottom View of Manguinhos Rambla

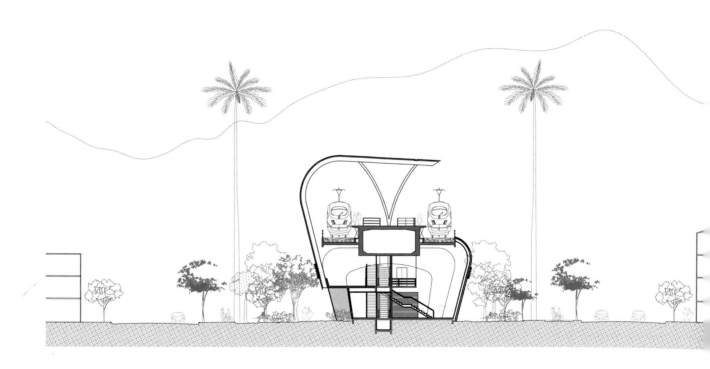

Manguinhos Rambla and train station sections

JORGE MARIO JÁUREGUI / METRÓPOLIS PROJECTOS URBANOS

Manguinhos Rambla under construction

MANGUINHOS COMPLEX

METRO CABLE

Caracas, Venezuela
2007–10

Urban-Think Tank

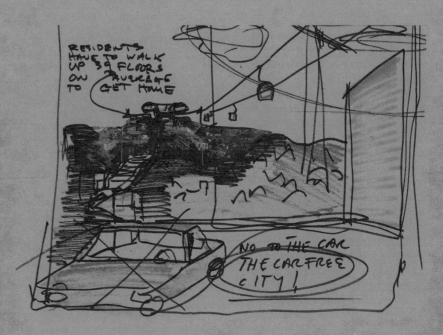

RESIDENTS HAVE TO WALK UP 50 FLOORS ON AVERAGE TO GET HOME

NO TO THE CAR
THE CAR FREE CITY!

Concept sketch

Venezuela's rapid economic development in the 1970s and '80s made its capital, Caracas, a chief magnet for the influx of poor, rural migrants. The explosive growth of its barrios has also meant that Caracas has one of highest percentages of improvised settlements in Latin America today; of its roughly five million inhabitants, an estimated sixty percent live in barrios. These areas suffer from many of the same problems as similar communities elsewhere: high rates of extreme poverty, inadequate infrastructure, and lack of public space, among others.

Providing the barrios access to public transportation, however, presents special challenges, given Caracas's mountainous terrain. Many of the barrios occupy the hills around the city center, and for this reason they are generally poorly connected to the bus and metro systems that service other sections of the city. Because of this the majority of their inhabitants are forced to make long and often arduous journeys on foot or arrange for private carpooling. In 2003 architects Alfredo Brillembourg and Hubert Klumpner, founding partners of the firm Urban-Think Tank, offered a bold solution to this problem. Within the framework of a major Caracas study, Urban-Think Tank proposed building a cable car to link the barrios La Vega and Petare, which abut the inner city, to the urban transportation system. Their idea marked a radical departure from the strategy previously embraced by the city's planning officials, who

had wanted to gradually link the barrios to the city by building new streets (to accommodate public buses), which would have meant demolishing large numbers of makeshift dwellings and drastically altering the barrios' configurations. A cable car, on the other hand, would require only selective intrusion into the social system and minimal damage to existing structures. At the same time, it would offer a highly effective means of transportation on the steep terrain.

After long discussions with political decision-makers and studies of the technical feasibility of such a link, the cable car was determined to be the best way to tie the barrios to the inner city. President Hugo Chávez personally embraced the concept, and in May 2006 set up a joint venture with an Austrian firm that specializes in the development of cable cars in mountainous settings as a step toward realizing a number of cable cars throughout the city. The first line to be built was for the barrio San Agustín, which is cut off from the city and a nearby metro station in the valley below by a multilane thruway—one of the city's main traffic arteries. The line would be just over a mile (1.8 kilometers) long, and the state-run Metro de Caracas, which would be able to establish a direct underground link between the cable car and the Parque

Central metro station, was engaged as the future operator of the system.

In 2007 Urban-Think Tank was officially commissioned to design the link. The firm's first proposal for San Agustín would not only tie the barrio to the city and its metro system by way of several different stations, but clustered around these stops would also be a variety of cultural spaces—a music school, a dance school, a library—that would make the areas new hubs of activity. Brillembourg and Klumpner also proposed building a number of sports facilities for the area. A design concept by the Swiss designer Ruedi Baur would give the entire system a look exclusively its own, from colored illumination on the station buildings to the lettering on the gondolas.

The cornerstone for the first station, which was the connection station to the metro, was laid in April of that same year. The occupants of the dwellings in the way of the mountain stations first had to be talked into moving to alternate housing. This was achieved by offering them compensation payments, yet negotiations dragged on. Given the complex planning and construction process, a number of the architects' original ideas had to be altered. Some elements of the first plan, such as the proposed wind turbines atop the mountain stations, the cultural facilities to be created in the stations, and even the graphic concept, were subjected to changes or postponed to some later date. Construction of all five stations was completed in late 2009, and regular service was begun in January 2010. The library planned for La Ceiba station (including a soccer field on its roof), which is the central stop of the three hillside stations, is already under construction, and the cultural facilities at the other stations are slated for construction and will be opened at a later date. More amenities, such as small supermarkets and community centers, are also being planned for inclusion in the hillside stations.

Despite the fact that in many respects the overall program could only be realized in limited form, Metro Cable successfully ties San Agustín to the city below. Some 40,000 barrio dwellers have access to it, and approximately 15,000 riders can be accommodated each day. The mountain stations offer magnificent views of the city, and in time are sure to attract others. Most importantly, however, residents from the hill's higher reaches, who once faced the long, challenging treks into the city, can now enjoy a swift connection to the metro and other components of the city's infrastructure. Along with the other positive benefits, this will contribute greatly to gradual changes in the barrio's social structure and provide it with new opportunities. Urban-Think Tank's design is already serving as the model for Metro Cable Mariche, another line being built by Metro Caracas, that will connect an even larger area of barrios to the city's metro system. That project is scheduled for completion in 2012.

—AL

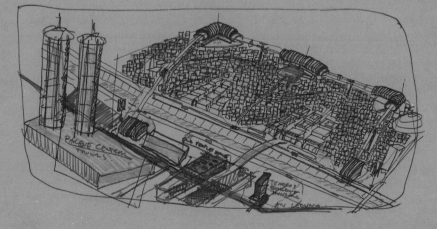

Concept sketch

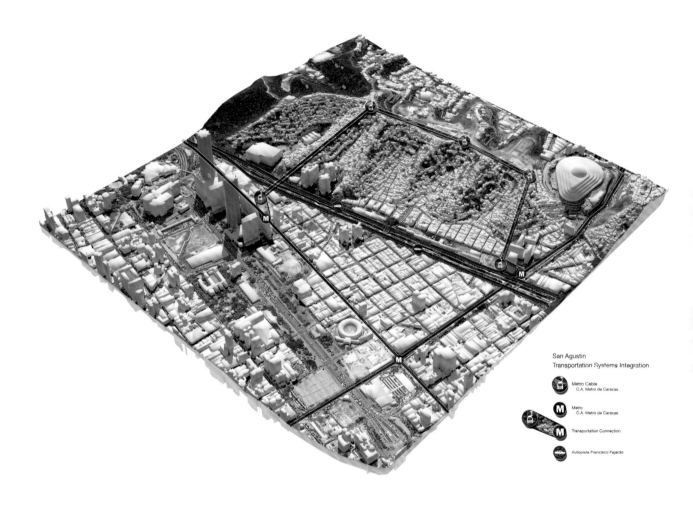

San Agustin
Transportation Systems Integration

Metro Cable
C.A. Metro de Caracas

Metro
C.A. Metro de Caracas

Transportation Connection

Autopista Francisco Fajardo

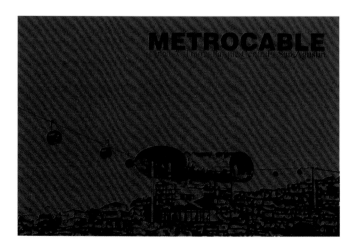

METROCABLE

Top Site perspective with transit diagram
Bottom Cover of proposal for Metro Cable

Following spread
Aerial view of Caracas with Barrio San
Agustín at far right

URBAN-THINK TANK

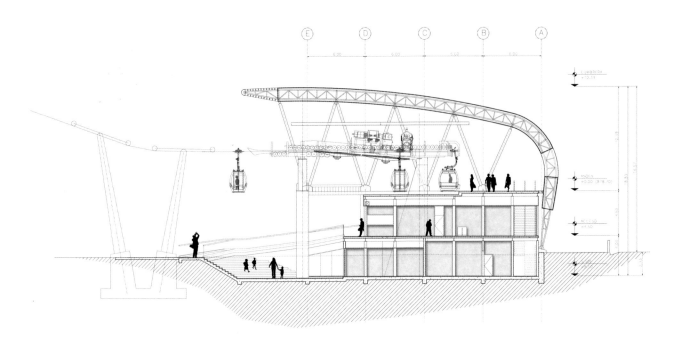

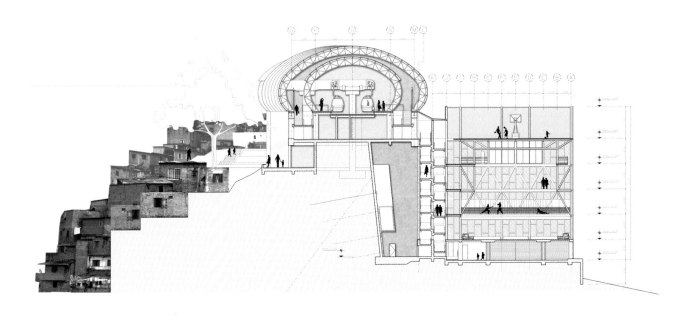

This page
Top San Agustín station section
Bottom La Ceiba station section

Facing page
Top San Agustín station exterior
Bottom La Ceiba station interior

URBAN-THINK TANK

Views from El Manguito station toward the city

View of Hornos de Cal station, old path at left

URBAN-THINK TANK

Project Credits

METI – Handmade School
Rudrapur, Bangladesh
2004-06
Anna Heringer
Linz, Austria

Primary School
Gando, Burkina Faso
1999-2001
Diébédo Francis Kéré
Berlin, Germany

Realization
Anna Heringer and Eike Roswag

Landscape design
Diébédo Francis Kéré

Engineers
Christof Ziegert, Uwe Seiler (structural engineers)

Construction
Residents of Gando

Consultants
Paul Tigga (development consultant); Prodip
Francis Tigga (pedagogy); Emmanuel and
Stefanie Heringer (bamboo experts and trainers);
Roland Gnaiger, Peter Kugelstätter, Oskar
Pankratz, Martin Rauch, Rudolf Sackmauer
(diploma consultants); Afsar Ali, Zainab
Faruqui Ali, BASEhabitat, Clemens Bernhardt,
BRACuniversity, Sepal Depsharwa, Jean Dethier,
Christiane Eickhoff, Dominique Gauzin-Müller,
Tobias Hagleitner, Saif Ul Haque, Karoline
Heinzle, Josef Heringer, Kurt Hörbst, Housing
and Building Research Institute Bangladesh,
Institute of Architects Bangladesh, Khondaker
Hasibul Kabir, Christine Karl, Edith Karl, Nahas
Khalil, Stefan Lang, Christiane Liebert, Fuad
Mallick, Stefan Neumann, Clemens Quirin, Petra
Rager, Swapan Saha, Montu Ram Shaw, Marina
Tabassum, Gunar Wilhelm; Christof Ziegert
(cob expert)

Client
Village of Gando, Burkina Faso;
Schulbausteine für Gando e.V.

Construction
Anna Heringer; Eike Roswag; Emmanuel and
Stefanie Heringer; craftsmen of Rudrapur

Client
NGO Dipshikha with Partnerschaft Shanti-
Bangladesh e.V. and Paepstliches Missionswerk
der Kinder

Housing for the Fishermen of Tyre
Tyre, Lebanon
1998-2008
Hashim Sarkis A.L.U.D.
Cambridge, Massachusetts /
Beirut, Lebanon

Design Team
Hashim Sarkis (architect); Ezra Block, Ryan Bollom, Cynthia Gunadi, Scott Hagen, David Hill, Ziad Jamaleddine, Paul Kaloustian, Brian Mulder, Cheyne Owens, Erkin Ozay, Anuraj Shah, Mete Sonmez (collaborators)

Landscape design
Hashim Sarkis Architecture Landscape Urban Design

Engineers
Mohamed Chahine and Mounir Mabsout (structural engineers)

Construction
EBCO-BITAR

Client
Al Baqaa Housing Cooperative; Association for Development of Rural Areas in South Lebanon (ADR)

Red Location Museum of Struggle
Port Elizabeth, South Africa
1998-2005
Noero Wolff Architects
Cape Town, South Africa

Design Team
Jo Noero (architect); Heinrich Wolff; Robert McGiven, Avish Mistry, Amit Patel, Tanzeem Razak, Ricardo Sa (collaborators); John Blair Architects (site architects)

Landscape design
Noero Wolff Architects

Engineers
CA Du Toit Eastern Cape (mechanical and electrical engineers); deVilliers & Hulme (structural and civil engineers); Walters & Simpson (quantity surveyors)

Construction
Alfdav Construction in association with SBT Construction (Eastern Cape); residents of Red Location township

Client
Nelson Mandela Metropolitan Municipality

Inner-City Arts
Los Angeles, California
1993-2008
Michael Maltzan Architecture
Los Angeles, California

Design team
Michael Maltzan (lead architect); Tim Williams (project director); Stacy Nakano (project manager); Owen Tang (project architect); Brian Cavanaugh, David Freeland, Brad Groff, Yvonne Lau, Ed Ogosta, Nadine Quimbach, Kurt Sattler, Krista Scheib, Jeff Soler (collaborators); Marmol Radziner and Associates (associate architects for Phase I)

Landscape design
Nancy Goslee Power & Associates, Inc.

Engineers
Innovative Engineering Group, Inc. (mechanical, electrical, and plumbing engineers); John A. Martin & Associates, Inc. (structural engineers); Paller-Roberts Engineering, Inc. (civil engineers)

Consultants
Entertainment Lighting Services (theater lighting); Martin Newson & Associates LLP (acoustics); Ph.D (signage and graphics)

Construction
Matt Construction

Client
Inner-City Arts

$20K House VIII
Newbern, Alabama
2009
Rural Studio, Auburn University
Newbern, Alabama

Quinta Monroy Housing
Iquique, Chile
2003–05
Elemental
Santiago, Chile

Casa Familiar: Living Rooms
at the Border and Senior Housing
with Childcare
San Ysidro, California
2001–present
Estudio Teddy Cruz
San Diego, California

Design team
Charity Bulgrien, Ian Cook, Obi Elechi (student team); Daniel Splaingard and Danny Wicke (instructors); Andrew Freear (program director)

Consultants
Paul Stoller – Atelier Ten (environmental consultant); Joe Farruggia – GFGR Architects & Engineers (structural engineering consultant); Xavier Vendrell – School of Architecture at University of Illinois at Chicago, Xavier Vendrell Studio (design consultant)

Project sponsor
Regions Bank

Client
David Thornton

Design team
Alejandro Aravena, Emilio de la Cerda, Tomás Cortese, Andrés Iacobelli, Alfonso Montero (architects)

Engineers
Alejandro Ampuero, Mario Alvarez, Juan Carlos de la Llera, Tomás Fischer, José Gajardo, Carl Lüders

Construction
Loga S.A.

Client
Gobierno regional de Tarapacá; Programa Chile-Barrio del Gobierno de Chile

Design team
Teddy Cruz (architect); Mark Clowdus, Cesar Fabela, Mark Gusman, Brian Jaramillo, Stella Robitaille, Megan Willis (present collaborators); Giacomo Castagnola, Adriana Cuellar, Andrea Dietz, Jesus Fernando Limon, Mariana Leguia, Gregorio Ortiz, Alan Rosenblum, Jota Samper, Nikhil Shah, Rastko Tomasevic (past collaborators)

Landscape Design
Leslie Ryan

Engineers
Envision Engineering: Alex Barajas (structural engineer)

Construction
TBD

Client
Casa Familiar

Transformation of Tour Bois-le-Prêtre
Paris, France
2006–11
**Frédéric Druot, Anne Lacaton,
and Jean Philippe Vassal
Paris, France**

Manguinhos Complex
Rio de Janeiro, Brazil
2005–10
**Jorge Mario Jáuregui /
Metrópolis Projetos Urbanos
Rio de Janeiro, Brazil**

Metro Cable
Caracas, Venezuela
2007–10
**Urban-Think Tank
Caracas, Venezuela /
New York, New York**

Design team
Frédéric Druot, Anne Lacaton, Jean Philippe Vassal (architects); Adis Tatarévic, Miho Nagashima, Florian de Pous, Mario Bonilla, Maria de Oliveira, David Pradel, Caroline Stahl (collaborators)

Engineers
Inex (systems engineers); VP & Green (structural engineers)

Consultants
E.2.I (cost consultant); Jourdan (acoustics); Vulcanéo (fire security consultant)

Construction
Batscop (construction coordinators)

Client
Paris Habitat

Design team
Jorge Mario Jáuregui (architect), Ana Luiza Sampaio, Maurício Santos, Fabiana Matos, Flavio Nunes, Marcelo Fernandes (collaborators)

Landscape design
Jorge Mario Jáuregui

Engineers
Arte Pontes Consultoria and S. F. Engenharia (structural engineers)

Construction
Consórcio Manguinhos

Client
Empresa de Obras Públicas do Estado do Rio de Janeiro (EMOP)

Design team
Alfredo Brillembourg and Hubert Klumpner (project design architects); José Antonio Nuñez, Carlos Bastidas, Alfredo Brillembourg, Patrick Edlinger, Elizabeth Florian, Cesar Gavidia, Dora Kelle, Hubert Klumpner, Rafael Machado, Claudia Ochoa, Regina Orvañanos, Juan Ponce, Matt Tarczynski (conceptual design team); Michael Contento, Lindsey Sherman (Metro Cable research, design, and exhibition)

Landscape design
Topotek 1: Christian Bohne, Martin Rein-Cano

Construction and project management
Constructora Norberto Odebrecht S.A. (CNO)

Engineers
DAC: Deleida Alvarez (project m/e/p coordination and project shop details), Carlos Silva (site supervision and project shop details); Doppelmayr

Seilbahnen GmbH: Martin Schöffel (interurban ropeway system); Eduardo Lopez (structural design project); Robert Silman Associates: Pat Arnett (structural design concept)

Project consultants
Felix Caraballo (community outreach); Intégral Ruedi Baur & Associés: Ruedi Baur (graphic design)

Client
C.A. Metro de Caracas: Cesar Nuñez

Credits

Acknowledgments

Every exhibition begins as an idea, and needs the help and advice of many people to get realized. This exhibition and catalogue have relied on the support of many colleagues, experts, and friends from both inside and outside of the Museum. First and foremost, my greatest thanks go to Glenn D. Lowry, Director of The Museum of Modern Art; Jennifer Russell, former Senior Deputy Director for Exhibitions, Collections, and Programs; Ramona Bannayan, Deputy Director for Exhibitions; and Peter Reed, Senior Deputy Director for Curatorial Affairs, for their support of this undertaking. I am deeply grateful to Barry Bergdoll, The Philip Johnson Chief Curator of Architecture and Design, for his support of this project from the very beginning, and for his rigorous guidance and unequaled advice through every phase of the project's planning.

I wish to thank The International Council for its generous funding of this exhibition, and the Patricia Cisneros Travel Fund for Latin America for its research and travel support. I would also like to thank Jay Levenson, Director of the International Program, and his team for their help.

Together with Margot Weller, Curatorial Assistant, Department of Architecture and Design, I would like to extend my deepest gratitude to the architects included in this exhibition and publication for their stalwart support, critical insights, and unquantifiable contributions: Alejandro Aravena; Alfredo Brillembourg and Hubert Klumpner; Frédéric Druot, Anne Lacaton, and Jean Philippe Vassal; Teddy Cruz; Andrew Freear (Rural Studio); Anna Heringer; Jorge Mario Jáuregui; Diébédo Francis Kéré; Michael Maltzan; Jo Noero; and Hashim Sarkis. Their ideas, conversation, and participation in developing this project have been invaluable. (Our sincere thanks, too, to some of the architects for accommodating memorable visits to their projects near and far.) We also thank this highly talented group for lending not only their models, drawings, and photographs but also their critical and innovative ideas, and, in some cases, the production of material ex novo. We would also like to extend our warmest thanks to the teams behind each of the architects, without whose continued correspondence and dedication this project would not have come together. Particular thanks to Claudia Buhmann (Kere Architecture); Marielly Casanova, Michael Contento, and Lindsey Sherman (Urban-Think Tank); Stacie Escario (Michael Maltzan Architecture); Cynthia Gunadi (Hashim Sarkis A.L.U.D.); Victor Oddó (Elemental); Lauren Oliver (Noero Wolff Architects); Stella Robitaille and Megan Willis (Estudio Teddy Cruz); and Danny Wicke (Rural Studio). Thanks also to Ph.D, a Design Office; Nancy Goslee Power & Associates; and Cité de l'architecture for their generous contributions. We offer very special thanks to Harun Farocki and his team for allowing us to include his beautiful film *In Comparison* in the exhibition. Further, our sincere appreciation goes to Iwan Baan, whose unmatched interest in this subject has strengthened both the publication and the exhibition immensely. Our thanks also go to all of the photographers whose work helps to bring these beautiful projects to life. We would like to thank Cameron Sinclair and Sarah Bush of Architecture for Humanity; Jörg Stollmann and Rainer Hehl of Urbaninform.net; and John Peterson and Liz Ogbu of The 1% for Architecture for their unique contributions to the exhibition. We are also grateful to Pablo Castro, Jennifer Lee, and Shin Kook Kang for help with the production of new models for the exhibition.

In preparing the concept and selection of the projects for this exhibition, a large number of people were involved in formative discussions. First and foremost is Fabienne Hoelzel, who shared with me her great knowledge and experience. More help and ideas came from Filipe Balestra and Sarah Göransson, Ute Meta Bauer, Bryan Bell, Adrian Blackwell, Olivier Boucheron, Emilio Caravatti, Gabriela Carrillo, Joe Dahmen, Oliver Elser, Jesko Fezer, Lisa Findley, Eva Maria Froschauer, Mary Graham, Joseph Grima, Zvi Hecker, Susanne Hofmann, Matthias Hollwich, Sarah Ichioka, Kathryn Kanjo, Olympia Kazi, Anupama Kundoo, Monte Laster, Andrea Lipps, Rafael Magrou, Giancarlo Mazzanti, Cara McCarty, Matilda McQuaid, Rahoul Mehrotra, William Menking, Baerbel Mueller, Enrique Norten, Rita Palma, Luis Pérez-Oramas, Vanja Petrovic, Ronald Rael, Martin Rauch, Rory Riordan, Philipp Rode, Beth Stryker, Simone Swan, Kai Vöckler, Wilfried Wang, Christian Werthmann, and Lynette Widder, among others. In my effort to enumerate all of the names deserving of recognition, there are undoubtedly oversights.

The Museum's Department of Publications, led by Christopher Hudson, has been an extraordinary team with which to work. Associate Publisher Kara Kirk and Editorial Director David Frankel have helped immensely in pushing forward this publication. The beautifully reproduced images included here are thanks to the astute eye of Production Director Marc Sapir, who also worked tirelessly to keep the many components of this volume on schedule. I am deeply thankful to Libby Hruska, Editor, who as a patient and thoughtful critic and adviser steered the book's texts into their final form. Our thanks to Sam Cate-Gumpert, Carole Kismaric Mikolaycak Intern in Publishing, for making sense of a labyrinthine series of project credits. For the book's thoughtful design, we are grateful to Adam Michaels, Prem Krishnamurthy, and Molly Sherman from Project Projects. Thanks, too, to our very skillful mapmaker, Adrian Kitzinger.

We would also like to thank colleagues around the Museum who have been involved in various aspects of the exhibition. I thank Kim Mitchell, Director of Communications, and Paul Jackson, Publicist, for getting the press interested in this show, and Todd Bishop, Director, Exhibition Funding, and his team for securing funding. Particular thanks go to Maria DeMarco Beardsley, Coordinator of Exhibitions, and Randolph Black, Associate Coordinator of Exhibitions, for their expert management of logistics related to this project. Assistant Registrar Allison Needle skillfully orchestrated the registration of all loans, organizing the safe transport of objects from four continents. We are grateful to Betty Fisher, Exhibition Designer, for pulling together the show's materials into a form that creatively balances the various positions represented and celebrates the overall spirit of the project. Very special thanks to Ingrid Chou, Assistant Director, Department of Graphic Design, for her work in shaping the visual identity of the exhibition. The project is further indebted to many across the Museum, including Nancy Adelson and Henry Lanman, General Counsel; Laura Beiles, Sara Bodinson, Pablo Helguera, and Wendy Woon, Department of Education; Karl Buchberg, Jim Coddington, Margo Delidow, Roger Griffith, and Erika

Mosier, Department of Conservation; Allegra Burnette, Shannon Darrough, Howard Deitch, Mike Gibbons, David Hart, Charlie Kalinowski, K Mita, and Matias Pacheco, Department of Information Technology; Claire Corey, Department of Graphic Design; Lauren Stakias, Department of Development and Membership; and Jeri Moxley, CETech.

The Department of Architecture and Design, expertly led by Barry Bergdoll, has provided immense support for this project. Special mention goes to Whitney May, Department Assistant, and Emma Presler, Department Manager, for their help with planning and programming associated with the exhibition. Thanks, too, to my estimable colleagues Paola Antonelli and Juliet Kinchin for their ongoing support and advice. Additionally, several very talented interns worked on this project, helping with all facets of the research, planning, and production phases: Iben Falconer, whose formative contributions in the early stages of planning are reflected in all facets of the project; James Green; Robert Wiesenberger; and Sarah Cloonan.

My special thanks and profound appreciation go to Margot Weller for all of her efforts and for the energy she put into the exhibition and this catalogue since the beginning of this project. She has been a critical respondent to all discussions, guiding and moderating a complex planning process to a very successful end. She also contributed a number of project texts to the catalogue and has been the indispensable bridge between all actors in preparing both this publication and the exhibition it accompanies.

My deepest gratitude goes to my wife, Cristina Steingräber, for her ongoing support of my work and ideas, and to my son, Maximilian,

who has just spent one year in India helping to bring change to the underserved Bhils tribal community.

Andres Lepik
Curator, Department of Architecture and Design